Poetry Therapy

Theory and Practice

Poetry Therapy
Theory and Practice

By
Nicholas Mazza, Ph.D., R.P.T.

Routledge
Taylor & Francis Group
www.routledgementalhealth.com

Published in 2003 by
Brunner-Routledge
29 West 35th Street
New York, NY 10001
www.brunner-routledge.com

Published in Great Britain by
Brunner-Routledge
27 Church Road
Hove, East Sussex
BN3 2FA
www.brunner-routledge.co.uk

Brunner-Routledge is an imprint of the Taylor & Francis Group.
Printed in the United States of America on acid-free paper.

10 9 8 7 6 5 4 3 2

Library of Congress Cataloging-in-Publication Data

Mazza, Nicholas.
    Poetry therapy : theory and practice / by Nicholas Mazza.
        p. cm.
Includes bibliographical references and index.
  ISBN 0-415-94486-4 (pbk.)
  1. Poetry—Therapeutic use. I. Title.

RC489.P6M393 2003
615.8′515—dc21   2002154332

Contents

Part four. Research and professional development

Appendices

Foreword

The therapeutic power of poetry has been known since ancient times. Yet, a comprehensive exploration of poetry therapy in a single volume has been missing until now. Instead, scholars and clinicians interested in the prevention and treatment aspects of poetry have focused their attention in one of two directions. Either they have written on particular aspects of the use of poetry as therapy with select populations or they have edited volumes of scholarly essays that, while interesting, have been sometimes uneven in their coverage. In *Poetry Therapy: Interface of the Arts and Psychology*, Nicholas Mazza advances the art and science of poetry therapy to a new height by providing a comprehensive treatment of the field from its history to its present development and future.

Mazza is uniquely qualified to bring together the various dimensions of poetry therapy. He has been an associate of some of the profession's founders, including Jack Leedy and Art Lerner. He was in attendance at many of the Association for Poetry Therapy conferences in the 1970s and was present at the incorporation of the National Association for Poetry Therapy in 1981. Mazza has also been the gatekeeper of the profession, serving as the editor of the *Journal of Poetry Therapy* since 1987. He has used poetry in a variety of therapeutic settings and has studied it extensively as a professor. In addition, Mazza is a first-rate poet. Therefore, it is not surprising that the contents of this book reflect a blending of a man who is a pioneer, a clinician, a scholar, and an artist.

Highlights of *Poetry Therapy* are numerous but include:

- The best history of the field yet written
- Extensive coverage of the research base of poetry therapy
- Specific chapters on using poetry therapy with individuals, groups, and families
- Coverage of how poetry may be employed therapeutically and developmentally with special populations most amenable to its use, such as children, adolescents, battered women, and the elderly

Mazza has written a practical as well as scholarly book. His examples of what poems to use in certain situations show a skill and provide a service rarely found in clinical texts. Mazza's illustrations of collaborative, dyadic, and individual poems, as well as his case examples, make this text come alive. The reader gets a feel for what the poetry therapy process is like, not just a description of it. The references section at the end of the book is an invaluable resource for finding the seminal works in the field. In addition, the appendices provide the reader with poems frequently used in therapy as well as different types of writing exercises and protocols to use in a variety of settings.

Overall, Nicholas Mazza has provided in *Poetry Therapy* the best of what the field has been, is, and will be. This book is a breakthrough in the literature because of its complete coverage of poetry as an art and a science in the healing of those who are mentally distressed and the helping of those who need guidance and inspiration to find their way in life. Like a playful but mature child, this book is a delight!

Samuel T. Gladding, Ph.D.
Professor of Counselor Education
Wake Forest University
Winston-Salem, North Carolina

Preface

Hope
Hope
is the belief
that one hand
reaching to another
can eventually
touch the moon,
allowing the light
to guide us
through the night.

—Nicholas Mazza

(Journal of Humanistic Education and Development, 36, 257, 1998.)

Introduction to the paperback edition

Poetry therapy touches and affirms our humanity
—NM

This paperback edition of *Poetry Therapy: Theory and Practice* (formerly, *Poetry Therapy: Interface of the Arts and Psychology*) is a primary text for those individuals with a particular interest in poetry therapy, writing and healing, bibliotherapy, and narrative therapy. This book was also designed to serve as a supplementary text for those interested in the broader area of arts therapies and the use of the arts in community practice. The change in title was based on feedback from readers who noted that the book was more than an *interface*. In fact, it provides a foundation for poetry therapy theory, practice, and research. Furthermore, the content, although inclusive of psychological material, extends to all of the helping professions, as well as literary scholars.

Poetry Therapy: Theory and Practice provides a multidimensional model of poetry therapy that can be used with a wide range of populations and applied in numerous settings. The R.E.S. (Receptive-Prescriptive/Expressive-Creative/Symbolic-Ceremonial) model is examined with respect to modalities (individual, family, group) and its use along developmental stages. A major purpose of this book is to help ground the practitioner and/or researcher in the fundamental principles and techniques of poetry therapy. Beyond the genre of poetry and any narrow definition of therapy, the emphasis is on the *poetic* and *therapeutic* elements involved in helping and educational endeavors. Of course, any individual using poetry therapy must first recognize the boundaries of his/her professional domain and adhere to appropriate practice/scholarship/ethical standards.

It is indeed an exciting and promising time to be involved with poetry therapy. The National Association for Poetry Therapy (NAPT) continues to grow and attract diverse and international interest. I am pleased and honored that this paperback edition is being published in response to the demand from practitioners, educators, students, and the general public. As with poetry and therapy, this book is unfinished. If it proves to be of some merit, then the reader will find something to apply, evaluate, build upon, and improve. May our journey toward practice excellence in poetry therapy find us crossing paths with old friends and making new ones as we move toward interdisciplinary dialogue and collaboration.

Nicholas Mazza

Introduction

It is common knowledge that psychology is both an art and a science. The depth of human experience (cognitive, affective, and behavioral domains) is best addressed by drawing from the humanities and sciences. Fowler (1998) noted the long history of the relationship between the arts and psychology, including the establishment of Division 10, "Psychology and the Arts", as a charter division of the American Psychological Association (APA) in 1945.

Poetry therapy, as one of the expressive arts therapies, includes attention to verbal and nonverbal behavior, language, symbolism, use of sensory modes, vision, order, and balance (Mazza, 1988). The emerging narrative-based psychotherapies (see, for example, White and Epston, 1990) have similar characteristics as clients are guided to conceptualize their contextual struggles. So it is with poetry therapy.

While one might argue that poetry therapy is not "mainstream" in the field of psychology, a careful review of the poetic in various APA divisions (e.g., humanistic psychology and family psychology), theoretical frameworks (e.g., psychoanalytic, Gestalt, cognitive), and practice models will show that elements of poetry therapy are widespread. In this book, poetry therapy will be considered one of the psychological methods that can be used in individual, family, and group therapies.

Poetry can be defined with respect to literary genre or the qualities or aspects of language that create an emotional response. The emphasis is on evocative language. Poetry therapy involves the use of the language arts in therapeutic capacities. In addition to the clinical use of preexisting poems in various modalities, the purview of poetry therapy includes bibliotherapy, narrative psychology, metaphor, storytelling, and journal writing (Mazza, 1993).

Drawing from an interdisciplinary base, this book is organized along three dimensions. The first dimension addresses the theory and practice of poetry therapy. Chapter one examines the historical and theoretical foundations for poetry therapy. Chapter two provides a poetry therapy practice model that contains three major components: (1) receptive/prescriptive mode, (2) expressive/creative mode, and (3) symbolic/ceremonial mode. These three components are designed to address the range of human experience. Specific techniques for each mode are delineated. Case illustrations for individual treatment conclude the chapter. Chapters three and four examine poetry therapy in family and group therapies, respectively.

The second dimension of this book addresses poetry therapy with four at-risk groups. Chapter five focuses on the use of poetry therapy with children, with specific attention paid to child abuse. Chapter six looks at adolescent suicide. Chapter seven deals with battered women. Chapter eight addresses the use of poetry therapy with the elderly.

The final dimension of this book looks at research and professional issues. Chapter nine examines the research base for poetry therapy and sets forth an agenda for the next millennium. Chapter ten addresses professional issues and examines the growing field of poetry therapy. This includes a look at credentialing, education, supervision, interdisciplinary and international involvement, resource development, and a vision.

The author

Nicholas Mazza, Ph.D., R.P.T., is a Professor of Social Work and Chairperson of the Arts and Community Practice Certificate Program at Florida State University, Tallahassee, FL. Dr. Mazza holds Florida licenses in psychology, clinical social work, and marriage and family therapy. He has been involved in the practice, research, and teaching of poetry therapy for 27 years. Dr. Mazza is the founding (1987) and current editor of the *Journal of Poetry Therapy: The Interdisciplinary Journal of Practice, Theory, Research, and Education*. He is past vice president and current board member of the National Association for Poetry Therapy (NAPT). In 1997, Dr. Mazza received the "Pioneer Award" from NAPT.

In addition to poetry therapy, Dr. Mazza has practiced, taught, and published in the areas of crisis intervention, death and trauma, family therapy, group work, clinical theories and models, and the arts in community practice. He is co-editor with Charles Figley and Brian Bride of *Death and Trauma: The Traumatology of Grieving* (1997, Taylor & Francis) and is a published poet.

Dr. Mazza is a member of the American Psychological Association (Division 10 Arts and Psychology), the National Association of Social Workers, the Council on Social Work Education, the American Counseling Association, and a Fellow in the American Orthopsychiatric Association. He has served on the editorial boards of *The Arts in Psychotherapy, Journal of Family Social Work, Journal for Specialists in Group Work, Social Work,* and the *Journal of Sociology and Social Welfare.*

Acknowledgments

This book encompasses a journey in poetry therapy that began in 1972 at Cumberland Hospital (Brooklyn, NY) with the 2nd Annual Association for Poetry Therapy Conference. Through the years I have been fortunate to become part of a network of friends in poetry therapy. I wish to especially acknowledge the late Arthur Lerner, pioneer and "Dean of Poetry Therapy" who was my friend, mentor, and colleague and who remains a guiding spirit. This book is also built upon the pioneering work of Jack J. Leedy and Arleen McCarty Hynes. I am grateful for their continued friendship and support. Two other close friends and colleagues deserve special mention, Samuel T. Gladding and Geri Giebel Chavis. Sam and Geri represent the highest standard in poetry therapy: scholarship with a heart. I would also like to thank my students and clients with whom I have shared a special journey.

A special thanks goes to Charles Figley, my friend and colleague at Florida State University. His encouragement, guidance, and support turned this book from a fantasy into a reality.

I am grateful to the staff at CRC Press for their support in publishing this manuscript: Barbara Norwitz, Senior Editor; Sarah Nicely Fortener, Project Editor; Carolyn Lea, Production Manager; Pat Roberson, Associate Production Manager; and Dennis McClellan. A special note of thanks also goes to Maggi Vanos-Wilson, Sherry Tointigh, and Delores Bryant for their technical assistance.

Finally I thank my family, friends, and all those who still believe that "the impossible dream" is possible and that there are "angels among us." Holding the hands of my children, Nicole and Christopher, I'm reminded that we carry our history, share our story, and look to the future. It's clear to me that with my children, I've experienced a poem that could never be written.

May the poem and this acknowledgment remain unfinished.

Dedication

To my children,
 Nicole and Christopher

And my father,
 Louis Salvatore Mazza (1914–2001)

And my mother,
 Catherine Giordano Mazza (1914–1995)

part one

Introduction

chapter one

The place of poetry therapy in psychology: historical and theoretical foundations

The pluralistic base of poetry therapy has evolved through the exploration and evaluation of the differential effects of the use of the poetic in a wide range of therapeutic capacities. Literary scholars have provided perspectives on the human condition which have been all too often neglected in the clinical literature. In *Striking at the Joints: Contemporary Psychology and Literary Criticism*, Knapp (1996) provided a text that can be used to advance the interface between the social sciences and the humanities. Going beyond the traditional literary criticism relating to Freudian theory, Knapp provides an analysis of contemporary psychology (e.g., cognitive theory) and literary works and criticism. Texts that have addressed both literary and clinical traditions include *Psychoanalyses, Psychology, and Literature: A Bibliography* (Kiell, 1990); *Life Guidance Through Literature* (Lerner and Mahlendorf, 1991); and *Youth Suicide Prevention: Lessons from Literature* and *The Aching Hearth: Family Violence in Life and Literature* (Deats and Lenker, 1989, 1991).

Building on literary and clinical traditions, the underlying assumption for this book is that, in poetry, form does not supersede content or function. Heightened emotions and compressed meaning are central to poetry (Brogan, 1993). Consistent with the romantic tradition, a verse form is not required to produce poetry. Nemoianu (1993, p. 1096), addressing romanticism, noted that "it was poetic language (whether in verse, in prose, or on the stage) that proved the most adequate medium for responding to modernity. It had the kind of variety and indeterminacy, richness, and flexibility that could make it privileged ground for experimenting with human potentialities and responses, redeeming the

3

past, assimilating the present, and projecting the future." With respect to intimacy and depth of meaning in literature, for romantic poets such as Wordsworth and Shelley there really was no boundary between poetry and prose (Brogan, 1993).

Cartwright (1996) discussed the power of the written word, noting that in his *Defense of Poetry* (1840) Shelley wrote that "every author is necessarily a poet, because language itself is poetry" (Shelley, cited in Cartwright, 1996, p. 390). Winchester (1916, p. 229) wrote that Shelley found the distinguishing element of poetry in its "power to reveal and illuminate." In his discussion of poetry and romanticism, Lacour (1993) noted that Wordsworth's definition of poetry in his *Preface to the Lyrical Ballads* (1800) was often only partially cited as "the spontaneous overflow of feelings." Lacour noted that Wordsworth also stated that poetry of value required the poet to think "long and deeply" (Wordsworth, cited in Lacour, 1993, p. 1086). Lacour argued that Wordsworth did not substitute feelings for knowledge, but rather bound them together. So it is with extreme positions taken on psychological theories and methods. Affective-based therapies are not void of cognition and behavior, cognitive theories are not void of affect, and so on. Rigor and discipline are essential to the merging of the arts and psychology.

Schneider (1998) argued that romantic perceptions have a long and unique place in the history of psychology, including the writings of William James. When Schneider examined the literary and artistic movement beginning in the late 18th century, he identified its individual and collective depth of the experience of humankind. He discussed the romantic influences on existential-humanistic, narrative, relational, and ecological psychologies. Central to a romantic approach to clinical practice is a concern for the human "lifeworld" featuring: (1) affect, imagination, and intuition; (2) holistic content; and (3) practitioner (investigator) as participant. Gergen (1994, p. 256) noted that "from a romanticist standpoint, to understand another is to experience in some manner, the other's subjectivity."

Poetry therapy reflects the classic issues in literary analysis and psychological practice: the romantic aspects of empathy and subjectivity vs. reason and observation. Gergen (1994) noted the parallel process between literary analysis and the empiricist tradition. In literary analysis, the focus is on the text or content rather than the human communication or form of presentation. In science, the focus is on "pure content" and "literal language"; yet, scientists collect and analyze data with "rhetorical forestructures through which the observational world is construed" (p. 41). Gergen gave an example of a mechanistic metaphor whereby a person's actions are defined in terms of stimuli and inputs, units, etc. In essence, the use of metaphor shapes how observations will be recorded and how the world view is constructed. As Gergen noted, concepts such as narrative and metaphor used in literary analysis can contribute to the development of psychological theory and practice. From a clinical perspective, Lerner (1987) stated that in poetry therapy the focus is on the person not the poem. Clients are not asked to identify the "true" meaning of a poem, but rather the personal meaning. Given the above link between literature (with a particular emphasis on romanticism) and psychology, the historical and theoretical foundations for poetry therapy will be examined.

Historical foundations

Ancient roots

Apollo, dual god of medicine and poetry, has often been referred to as a starting point for the historical foundation for poetry therapy (Brand, 1980; Leedy, 1969a; Morrison, 1969; Putzel, 1975). The ancient Greeks are credited with being one of the earliest people to intuitively conceive of the importance of words and feelings to both poetry and healing (Putzel, 1975).

In *Poetics*, Aristotle discussed the role of catharsis in effecting an emotional cure. The value of poetry in producing insights and providing universal truths was also noted (Weller and Golden, 1993). Today, catharsis is considered an important aspect of psychotherapy (Nichols and Zax, 1977), one of the therapeutic factors in group psychotherapy (Yalom, 1995), and a central component of psychodrama (Moreno, 1946, 1948, 1969). Emotional identification, the principal factor in catharsis, is also an important consideration with the use of poetry in therapeutic settings (Lessner, 1974).

Blinderman (1973) traced the use of poetry to deal with emotional problems even further in history to preliterate times when incantations and invocations were used. Often the purpose of the chanted word was to bring about change in self, others, or the environment. In his discussion of the American Indian, Astrov (1962, p. 207) noted the power of the word: "It is not the herb administered to the sick which is considered the essential part of the cure, rather the words recited over the herb before its use." This view is held universally by primitive healers (Blinderman, 1973; Frank, 1973). In *Persuasion and Healing*, Jerome Frank (1973) offered a more comprehensive discussion of the power of words, feelings, and beliefs in regard to curative functions.

Recent history

More recent history indicated that poetry was used for mental health purposes in the early 19th century. Jones (1969) noted that psychiatric patients were writing poems for the Pennsylvania Hospital newspaper, *The Illuminator*, in 1843. Bibliotherapists have noted that Benjamin Rush was the first American to recommend reading for the sick and the mentally ill in the early 1800s (Rubin, 1978a). Morrison (1973) found support for the curative function of poetry by pointing to the poet Robert Graves, who wrote in 1922 that "a well-chosen anthology is a complete dispensary for the more common mental disorders and may be used as much for prevention as for cure" (p. 79).

In 1925, Robert Haven Schauffler wrote *The Poetry Cure: A Pocket Medicine Chest of Verse*. The format of the book is prescriptive. Poems are provided for particular moods and problems. For example, one chapter (a collection of poems) is entitled "Sedatives for Impatience (Poems of Reassurance)". Schauffler also provides a section called "Directions (Read Well Before Using)". He cautions readers that poems do not affect everyone in the same way and to use them carefully. Another interesting point made in this book is that "any poem that has genuine healing in its wings usually commences its medical career the moment it is conceived by promptly curing its creator" (p. xviii). Central to this book are the points made by Schauffler regarding the value of both reading and writing poetry and his being a forerunner in pointing to the potential dangers of indiscriminate use of poetry. He was also a pioneer in providing a classification of poems according to 14 common complaints of his patients. In 1931, Schauffler's *The Junior Poetry Cure: A First-Aid Kit of Verse for the Young of All Ages* was published.

In his book, *The Poetic Mind*, Frederick Clark Prescott (1922) also noted the value of poetry as a safety valve for troubled individuals. Prescott, an English professor, had two articles relating to poetry and dreams published in the *Journal of Abnormal Psychology* (1912, 1919). *The Poetic Mind*, within a literary frame of reference and historical context, was a significant contribution to the linking of poetic thought with psychological principles.

Contemporary developments

The Healing Power of Poetry, by Smiley Blanton (1960), was another attempt at classification of poems for specific problems and moods. Blanton, a psychiatrist, discussed the therapeutic value of poetry and maintained a prescriptive approach often using inspirational poetry. Eli Griefer is credited with giving poetry therapy its name (Schloss, 1976). He was a poet, lawyer, and pharmacist who volunteered his time at Creedmoor State Hospital in New York. According to Schloss (1976), Griefer met with Jack J. Leedy, a psychiatrist, and together they developed a poetry therapy group. They also received support and encouragement from J.L. Moreno and were able to make presentations at the American Society for Group Psychotherapy and Psychodrama. Moreno was interested in the use of poetry in therapy and used the term "psychopoetry". This was to be later developed by Schloss (1976). In 1963, Griefer wrote *Principles of Poetry Therapy*. Leedy continued Griefer's work, and in 1969 edited an interdisciplinary collection of chapters in *Poetry Therapy: The Use of Poetry in the Treatment of Emotional Disorders* (Leedy, 1969b). In 1973, Leedy followed with a second edited volume, *Poetry the Healer* (Leedy, 1973). Chapters from both books were later published in *Poetry the Healer: Mending the Troubled Mind* (Leedy, 1985). Formal recognition of poetry therapy was evolving with the establishment of the Association for Poetry Therapy (APT) in 1969. Beginning in 1971, annual conferences were held in New York. In 1981, the APT became formally incorporated as the National Association for Poetry Therapy (NAPT). Since that time, annual conferences have been held at sites across the United States.

Gilbert Schloss made a significant contribution to poetry therapy with his work in psychopoetry. With a background in psychodrama, Schloss worked in New York out of the Institute for Sociotherapy, which provided workshops and educational experiences. In 1976, Schloss' *Psychopoetry* was published. He presented a number of case histories, including patient poems. Schloss also conducted a survey of approximately 1400 helping professionals to examine what poems were used for specific purposes. Only 194 questionnaires were returned. The respondents were mostly professionals involved with therapy (psychologists, social workers, counselors, etc.). The single largest group consisted of therapists working with individuals in private practice. Very few of the respondents classified themselves as poetry therapists. Schloss' initial purpose was to form a classification of poems with respect to therapeutic setting. He did not gain consensual validation for any of the poems in his classification of client moods, psychological states, and diagnostic categories. In addition to noting some of the methodological problems in his survey, Schloss observed that the wide variety of existing poetry and the newness of the field contributed to the problem. New directions were offered for further research, as well as a call for a vehicle to link many of the practitioners involved with poetry in therapy.

In Los Angeles, Arthur Lerner, a poet and psychologist, founded the Poetry Therapy Institute in 1973. This institute "was the first legally incorporated nonprofit organization devoted to the study and practice of poetry therapy" (Lerner, 1992, p. 107). The institute disbanded in 1992, but not before it made significant advancements in education and training in poetry therapy. *Poetry in the Therapeutic Experience* (Lerner, 1978; second edition published in 1994) provided a collection of chapters on practice, theory, and research. Of particular interest is Berry's "Approaching Poetry Therapy from a Scientific Orientation" which provided one of the first statistical studies in the field.

The Therapy of Poetry (Harrower, 1972) is also important in its consideration of poetry as therapy and being a part of normal development. Harrower reviewed her own journals and poems within a developmental framework, referring at times to Erik Erikson's (1963) stages of development. Her work is significant in that it provides a rationale for a health-based consideration of poetry in individual or group settings.

Bibliotherapy

Bibliotherapy developed out of the librarian tradition with its emphasis on recommended readings for particular problems or concerns. Carolyn Shrodes (1949), one of the pioneers in bibliotherapy, defined it as "the process of dynamic interaction between the personality of the reader and literature as a psychological field which may be used for personality assessment, adjustment and growth" (p. 28). Shrodes, from a psychoanalytic perspective, described a parallel process of client involvement in psychotherapy and literature. The process in both situations involves identification, catharsis, and insight. Rhea Joyce Rubin's two books, *Bibliotherapy: A Guide to Theory and Practice* (1978a) and *Bibliotherapy Source Book* (1978b) further advanced the field of bibliotherapy. *Biblio/Poetry Therapy: The Interactive Process* (Hynes and Hynes-Berry, 1986) served to provide an excellent text that differentiated "reading bibliotherapy" (prescriptive reading) from "interactive bibliotherapy" with a focus on "the triad of participant-literature-facilitator" (p. 11). With respect to clinical application, the terms "interactive bibliotherapy" and "poetry therapy" are essentially synonymous.

Theoretical

A significant portion of the theoretical foundation for the use of poetry in therapy is drawn from the psychoanalytic literature (e.g., Ansell, 1978; Parker, 1969; Pattison, 1973; Pietropinto, 1973). In Freudian theory, the unconscious, instinctual wishes and conflicts are responsible for both the production of fantasy and a literary work (Brenner, 1973). Brand (1980), in noting Freud's influence on writing and psychotherapy, stated (p. 54):

> "All in all, Freud's hypothesis that poetry and psychoanalysis shared the unconscious and preconscious materials of dreams and fantasies, his systematic self-analysis, and his audacious practice of correspondence as a therapeutic medium drew enduring attention to the unexplored potential of writing for psychological healing."

Díaz de Chumaceiro (1996, 1997, 1998) discussed the importance of prose and poetry in psychoanalytically oriented treatment with respect to unconsciously induced recall of poetry and prose. She noted that significant therapeutic benefits can be achieved by paying attention to literary processes that surface in the therapist's consciousness during treatment. Díaz de Chumaceiro (1997, p. 242) wrote: "Analyses of manifest and latent contents, as if a dream, of unconsciously induced recall of prose and poetry can serve to further understanding of patients' conflicts and resolve transference-countertransference resistances impeding progress."

The close connection between poetry and psychotherapy in Freudian terms is the mutual use of preconscious and unconscious material to explore inner feelings and the use of words to give it form. Both poetry and therapy are attempting the resolution of inner conflict. Symbolization and displacement are used in both cases. Pattison (1973, p. 212) wrote: "Because symbolization is the communicational vehicle for organizing, synthesizing, and representing the self, the poem as a symbolic vehicle is a potent mode of psychotherapeutic communication." Freud did not consider poetry as therapy; rather, he was interested in investigating the dimensions of the artist's personality (Robinson and Mowbray, 1969). He believed the origin of art was neurosis.

Jung was to redirect many of Freud's concepts and essentially moved from a cure model to a growth model (Putzel, 1975). Jung did not view art as disease nor did he view symbols as symptoms. For Jung, a symbol was something more than a term. It included an allusive element. He distinguished a symbol from a sign by referring to a sign as a direct representation of an object. Jung denoted responsibility to the poet for giving meaning to the poem as opposed to subjecting it to psychological analysis. Jung implicitly suggested that all people are poets and through various elements of creativity can develop a unique meaning system and world (Putzel, 1975). Whitmont and Kaufmann (1973, pp. 108–109) discussed art in the context of analytic psychology:

> "All too often, artistic products are analyzed reductively, traced to the family constellation of the artist, or to childhood traumata. Inspired art, however, is more than that: It is a personal expression of something universal and timeless, existing in each of us. ...Creativity involves the ability to give realistic and visible expression to archetypal form drives without being inundated by them. An artist ... does not create because he is neurotic, but may because he is creative and has to contend with powerful forces within himself."

While Freud was concerned with pathology, Jung viewed art more in terms of normality.

Adlerian psychology also offers some interesting concepts related to poetry therapy. Adler's concept of the individual's verbal-symbolic innate response potentialities is of particular importance. Adler viewed this response as the most important of the class of human responses (Ford and Urban, 1963). This takes on special significance in considering our basic methods of communicating needs, interests, and feelings. Through symbols and language we develop interpersonal relationships. An essential point in Adlerian theory is to understand the individual within a social context (Adler, 1954). His concept of the creative self recognizes the uniqueness of the individual pursuing experiences that are fulfilling. These experiences can be found in the social context or they can be created (Hall and Lindzey, 1978). The concept of fictional finalism is also relevant to this study. Adler maintained that people are motivated to a greater extent by their expectations of the future rather than past experience. People develop certain "fictions" they live by which are indicative of how the world is conceived and related to achieving goals. These fictions can be useful but need to be dismissed at points in time when demanded by reality. Perhaps this relates to Freud's conception of the poet alternating between reality and fantasy. The cognitive component of Adler's theory is consistent with functioning and developing in a social context and utilizing language or symbols to communicate.

Adler respected the poet's ability to understand a person's style of life. Adler (1933; cited in Ansbacher and Ansbacher, 1956, p. 329) noted that:

> "Their ability to show the individual living, acting, and dying as an indivisible whole in closest connection with the tasks of his environment raises our highest admiration. ...Some day it will be realized that the artist is the leader of mankind on the path to the absolute truth. Among poetic works of art which have led me to the insights of Individual Psychology the following stand out as pinnacles: fairy tales, the Bible, Shakespeare, and Goethe."

Similar to Freud, the poet received recognition for insights and sensitivities; however, Adler's focus was less intrapsychic and more interpersonal.

The humanistic foundation for the therapeutic use of poetry can be traced to Gestalt theory. In *Gestalt Therapy* by Perls, Hefferline, and Goodman (1951), there is a chapter on "Verbalizing and Poetry". The importance of language to relationships is noted, and poetry is clearly differentiated from neurotic verbalizing. Neurotic communication is described in terms of dissipating energy, while poetry is considered from a problem-solving perspective. In *Creative Process in Gestalt Therapy*, Zinker (1977) discussed creativity as an act of personal expression as well as a social act. In essence, life is a creative process. He refers to the structure and flow of each therapy session, which begins simply with a mutual sharing of awareness that eventually leads toward a meaningful theme. The theme is then developed and ultimately transformed into a new way of thinking or behaving. Zinker (1977) also referred to a central assumption of this study — the unfinished aspect of poetry. He wrote (p. 4):

> "A poem can be rewritten a thousand times, each attempt a new way of experiencing the process of one's thoughts. The new words themselves modify one's experience, one's ideas, words, and images. Analogies and metaphors move fluidly into one another like the conversation of good friends. Each rewritten poem, like each unit of an ongoing relationship, has its own internal validity."

Zinker (1977) drew a parallel between poetry and psychotherapy — both are involved in change and transformation. He viewed the therapist as an artist with the role of creating a therapeutic structure or atmosphere and beginning a process via the relationship. This process will ultimately promote self-exploration and growth. In considering the humanistic influence, it is also important to note the work of Maslow, who called for a new approach in psychotherapy based on the intensity of poets rather than a focus on pathology, and Jourard, who recognized the therapeutic value of literature (Brand, 1979).

The previous discussion has primarily involved theoretical orientations that primarily consider the individual. Moreno, considered by many as the father of group psychotherapy, has also made a significant contribution to the theoretical base of poetry therapy. As mentioned earlier in this text, Moreno used poetry in therapy before it received formal recognition, but he referred to it as psychopoetry (Schloss, 1976). Moreno's (1946, 1948, 1969) *Psychodrama* was a major influence in utilizing artistic methods in psychotherapy. Moreover, it was to affect group psychotherapy (a term he coined in 1932) by introducing such techniques as role-playing, the use of action, empathic identification, and catharsis (Shaffer and Galinsky, 1989). Both Gestalt and psychodramatic theory stressed the importance of role examinations and the use of metaphor.

Central works related to the theoretical foundations for poetry therapy include Freud's (1908/1959) "The Relation of the Poet to Day-dreaming" and Jung's (1922/1972) "On the Relation of Analytic Psychology to Poetry", as well as material from Adlerian (individual psychology), Gestalt, and psychodramatic theory.

More recently, narrative and constructivist therapies with an emphasis on language, symbol, and story also have a common base in poetry therapy. For example, Mince (1992, p. 321) noted that in family therapy the constructivist "paradigm shift moves the practice and theory of family therapy from a cybernetic base to a linguistic base." Witkin (1995), in presenting a "critical constructionist" perspective, noted the importance of language as a means of understanding clients and helping them redefine their situation in a manner that facilitates the attainment of their goals.

Writing and therapy

The historical and theoretical foundations for the use of writing in clinical practice have been well documented. Allport (1942) wrote *The Use of Personal Documents in Psychological Science*, legitimizing and advancing the use of diaries and journals in clinical practice. Landsman (1951) found that clients were better able to express their anxieties through writing rather than talking. Farber (1953) recognized the time-consuming limitations of using writing in therapy, however, and noted the advantage of slowing down the tempo of a session and providing a means to explore often ignored thoughts and feelings. Ellis (1955) described a variety of written forms as useful adjunctive techniques. Widroe and Davidson (1961) noted that directed writing in psychotherapy provides an enduring symbol and means for clients to examine and re-examine feelings associated with particular expressions. They also noted that writing is especially helpful with schizophrenic clients by providing a vehicle to express order and concreteness in their daily activities.

With the publication of *The Use of Written Communication in Psychotherapy* (Pearson, 1965), a number of applications of writing to clinical practice were explored. The book was a product of a symposium (The Uses of Written Communication in Counseling and Psychotherapy) sponsored by Psychologists Interested in the Advancement of Psychotherapy and held at the annual American Psychological Association convention. The most consistently cited advantage of using writing in psychotherapy was the provision of a vehicle to express and analyze emotion. The most consistent disadvantage cited was the provision of a vehicle to promote resistance through intellectualization and avoidance.

McKinney (1976, p. 183) noted that college students may write as a form of self-therapy "or at least an attempt at working out problems through displacement and sublimation in a socially acceptable form of fantasy." McKinney suggested that writing could have a cathartic effect by providing a release of strong feelings while under pressure. It could also serve to reduce internal conflict, anxiety, and confusion. Brand (1980) examined therapy in writing as a psychoeducational enterprise. She conducted a study on personal growth and creative writing with eighth-grade students. The variables examined were "student self-concept, student perception of problems, and depth of self-information" (p. 64). The results from objective measures comparing treatment and control groups indicated that the writing intervention was responsible for an increase in the provision of self-information; however, there were no significant differences with respect to self-examination. The impact on self-concept yielded mixed results. Brand also provided a descriptive analysis of the program and students, noting many of the peculiar aspects of growth not amenable to statistical evaluation (e.g., working through periods of confusion and changing styles of communication).

The emergence of constructivist and narrative approaches to clinical practice and research on emotional expression or trauma and writing have contributed to a stable base for the establishment of writing (written expression) as one of the major elements of poetry therapy. White and Epston (1990) advanced narrative therapy by providing a conceptual framework and the practical application of various writing techniques, particularly letters leading to the "externalization of the problem" and having clients "story" and "re-story" their lives. Building on the work of Jerome Brunner, the authors wrote (p. 217):

> "We would like to rest our case for a therapy that incorporates narrative and written means. We have found these means to be of very great service in the introduction of new perspective and to *a range of possible worlds*, to the privileging of vital aspects of lived experience in the *recreation* of unfolding states, in enlisting persons in the re-authoring of their lives and relationships."

Narrative therapy (Monk et al., 1997) and poetry therapy use language for therapeutic purposes. Drewery and Winslade (1997) noted that a philosophy of language stressing that meaning is determined by context (or that meaning is a social construction) is part of the foundation for narrative therapy. Although narrative therapy does not rely exclusively on written means, the "story" in its overall form is consistent with the overall traditions of poetry therapy.

There has been a significant body of literature indicating that emotional expression has a positive effect on mental and physical health and that emotional inhibition has negative effects (Smyth, 1998). The use of written expression in improving mental and physical health with respect to trauma has received support in numerous studies (e.g., Donnelly and Murray, 1991; Francis and Pennebaker, 1992; Lange, 1994; Murray and Segal, 1994; Pennebaker, 1993; Spera et al., 1994). In subsequent chapters, the therapeutic benefits of group writing in family and group therapies will also be addressed.

In summary, the place of poetry therapy in psychology is built on several foundations including romantic philosophy, traditional and contemporary psychological theories, interdisciplinary contributions, bibliotherapy, and research on the therapeutic effects of writing. Briefly defined, poetry therapy involves the use of the language arts in therapeutic capacities.

part two

Model and modalities

chapter two

Poetry therapy practice model and individual treatment

Elements of poetry therapy have been utilized with different methods in a variety of helping conditions. Use of literature, client writing, storytelling, and symbolic activities have all been utilized in clinical practice. The proposed poetry therapy practice model is an attempt at a comprehensive framework that accounts for the differential use of poetic techniques with a wide range of clients. As such, poetry therapy can be described in practical units and subjected to further clinical research.

The poetry therapy practice model proposed in this chapter includes three components:

1. The receptive/prescriptive component involving the introduction of literature into therapy
2. The expressive/creative component involving the use of client writing in therapy
3. The symbolic/ceremonial component involving the use of metaphors, rituals, and storytelling

All three components have the potential to address the cognitive, affective, and behavioral domains of human experience. As such, poetry therapy can be adapted to most psychological practice models. The following techniques are delineated for the practitioner with the caution that timing, appropriateness, and consistency with clinical purpose must be considered in their implementation.

Receptive/prescriptive: preexisting poems

One of the more common techniques used in poetry therapy is reading a poem to an individual or group (or having the client or clients read the poem) and inviting reactions. The therapist must anticipate and be willing to explore the client's reactions. Such a process should begin with the therapist examining his or her own reactions to the poem before using it in therapy. The introduction of the poem into the session could be connected with the content and dialogue of the session (see Table 1). For example, a client may express frustration about being "put off" in career and family matters. The words "put off" could be replaced with "deferred" or "lost hopes"; Langston Hughes' (1951/1970) poem "Harlem" deals with the possible outcomes of a dream being "deferred" and can be introduced to allow clients to make

Table 1 Table of Poems/Stories

Problem	Poem	Poet/author	Source
Decision making	"Road Not Taken"	Robert Frost	Lanthem[d]
Despair	"Hope Is a Thing with Feathers"	Emily Dickinson	Johnson[b]
Identity	"We Wear the Mask"	Paul Dunbar	Dore[c]
Intimacy	"If There Be Sorrow"	Mari Evans	Dore[c]
Internal conflict	"Flower in the Crannied Wall"	Alfred, Lord Tennyson	Dore[c]
Death of pet (for children)	*The Tenth Good Thing About Barney* (story)	Judith Viorst	Viorst[g]
Anger	*Anger* (fable)	J. Ruth Gendler	Gendler[e]
Love/authenticity	*The Velveteen Rabbit* (story)	Margery Williams	Williams[h]
Loss (for children)	*Everett Anderson's Goodbye* (story)	Lucille Clifton	Clifton[a]
Sexual assault	"Rape"	Marge Piercy	Piercy[f]

[a] Clifton, L. (1983) *Everett Anderson's Goodbye*, New York: Henry Holt & Co.

[b] Johnson, J.H., Ed. (1961) *Final Harvest: Emily Dickinson's Poems*, Boston: Little, Brown & Company.

[c] Dore, A., Ed. (1970) *The Premier Book of Major Poets*, Greenwich, CT: Faucett.

[d] Lathem, E.C., Ed. (1969) *The Poetry of Robert Frost*, New York: Holt, Rinehart & Winston.

[e] Gendler, J.R. (1984/1988) *The Book of Qualities*, New York: Harper Perennial.

[f] Piercy, M. (1990) *Circles on the Water: Selected Poems of Marge Piercy*, New York: Alfred A. Knopf.

[g] Viorst, J. (1971) *The Tenth Good Thing About Barney*, New York: Macmillan.

[h] Williams, M. (1975) *The Velveteen Rabbit*, New York: Avon.

an emotional identification with the poem. The poem can also serve as a springboard for them to talk about feelings, goals, and values (Mazza, 1979).

Questions relating to the poem should be directed in the manner of "What does it mean for you?" Reactions may focus on the poem as a whole or on a particular line or image — for example, "Is there any particular line that reached you or that you could call your own?" Clients can also be invited to modify the poem or provide a different ending. When possible, copies of the poem should be given to the clients so they has a visual reference.

Providing the lyrics of popular songs and playing an audiotape of the songs is another variation of this technique. The selection of poems or songs may be prescriptive and based on the principle of choosing a poem close in mood to that of the client but with a positive ending (Leedy, 1969c). Open-ended poems can facilitate self-exploration (Lessner, 1974). An example of such an open-ended poem would be Stephen Crane's (1895/1970) "If I Should Cast Off This Tattered Coat", which allows a client a wide range of reactions and conclusions. A prescriptive poem would be Kahlil Gibran's (1952) "On Marriage", which is instructive and implies a specific message. Clients can also be encouraged to bring to sessions a poem or song they have found particularly helpful.

Finally, clients can be asked about the poems or songs they like to read or listen to, across various moods. The relationship of the mood to the meaning of the song or poem can provide fruitful clinical information and self-understanding for the client.

The poetry/literature selection is one of the most difficult challenges faced by clinicians using poetry therapy. The issue of selection has been raised by several authors (Barron, 1973; Berry, 1978; Edgar and Hazley, 1969a; Hynes and Hynes-Berry, 1986/1994; Luber, 1976, 1978; Rolfs and Super, 1988; Rossiter et al., 1990; Schloss, 1976). Leedy's (1969c) isoprinciple of selecting a poem that matches the emotional state of the client but offers a positive ending may prove to be counterproductive if the clients perceive the positive ending as invalidating their feelings or reflecting the clinician's lack of sensitivity to the depth of client despair. Hynes and Hynes-Berry (1986/1994) offered detailed criteria for the selection of poetic material according to thematic dimensions (e.g., imagery, rhythm, and diction). Rolfs and Super (1988) identified the importance of the process of poetry selection and noted transference/countertransference issues. Rossiter, Brown, and Gladding (1990) studied the effect of poem selection on therapeutic process and outcome. They found that literature is more than a catalyst in the therapeutic process; the success or failure of a poem may depend on what the poem and therapist "ask" of a client.

Expressive/creative

Creative writing

The use of creative writing (poems, stories, diaries) is another useful technique for both assessment and treatment. It provides a vehicle for the client to express emotion and gain a sense of order and concreteness. The writing may be free writing (i.e., any topic, any form) or prestructured (i.e., specific instructions given on form or content). The use of sentence stems (such as "When I am alone..." or "If you knew me...") is a moderately structured format. In working with children, Koch (1970) offers numerous techniques. They include writing a poem in which every line begins with "I wish..." or using contrasting themes by alternating lines such as "I used to be.../But now...".

Clustering is another creative writing technique developed by Rico (1983) whereby an individual can free associate images to a central word such as "anxiety". With the central word encircled, the individual draws offshoots relating people, memories, feelings, places, etc. This exercise can then lead to creation of a poem. Adams (1990) found this technique to be particularly helpful in journal writing

Journal writing

Keeping a diary, log, or journal is another poetry therapy tool that serves to provide a vehicle for individuals to express thoughts and feelings in a meaningful and personal way. It can also provide some element of control to clients as they try to sort out difficult feelings in a confidential manner. The degree of prestructuring of journal entries relates to clinical purpose and client needs. There is a variety of forms of journal writing (see, for example, Adams, 1990; Baldwin, 1977; Progoff, 1975). The journal can range from simply being an open-ended recording of one's experiences to a highly structured log of thoughts and behaviors. The writer should always retain the right to share or not share the content of the journal with the clinician. Scrapbooks, autobiographies (Birren and Deutchman, 1991), and personal life history books (Kliman, 1990) are still other variations of journal writing. Each technique serves to provide some element of control and expressiveness to the client. Each has the potential to provide a historical perspective and perhaps a sense of connectedness.

Letter writing

The use of letter writing in therapy can be traced to Freud's practice of using correspondence as a therapeutic tool (Brand, 1979). Burnell and Motelet (1973) noted the use of "correspondence therapy" as an aid in dealing with physical distance, breaking resistance, and capitalizing on client strengths (e.g., creativity) or limitations (e.g., hearing-impaired clients). The availability of electronic mail further increases the therapeutic possibilities. A client can also be encouraged to write a letter (that may or may not be sent to a person) as a means of ventilating feelings.

Symbolic/ceremonial

Metaphors

The use of metaphors in therapeutic capacities has been addressed by numerous authors (see, for example, Barker, 1985; Erickson and Rossi, 1980; Gladding and Heape, 1987; Gordon, 1978; Lankton and Lankton, 1989; Pearce, 1996). In its most elemental sense, "a metaphor is something that stands for something else" (Combs and Freedman, 1990, p. xiv). Metaphors are symbols or images for emotions, actions, and beliefs.

Combs and Freedman (1990, pp. 90–91) offered some ways to find symbols for emotional states and attitudes:

1. List a dozen emotional states or attitudes (such as confidence, relaxation, indignation, and compassion) that might be useful in therapy.
2. Take the first item on your list and ask yourself, "If that state or attitude were a picture or image, what would it be a picture or image of?"
3. Wait for an image to occur to you. When an image has presented itself, make note of it on a separate piece of paper.
4. Then go back to the first item on your list. Ask yourself, "If that state or attitude were a physical posture or action, what posture or action would it be?" Make a note of the answer that you find.
5. Ask yourself, "If the state or attitude were a sound, what sound would it be?" List your answer beside your previous answers for this particular state or attitude.
6. Go through the same process with each of the other states or attitudes on your list. Each image, posture, and sound that you discover could be used as a symbol for the state or attitude.
7. Feel free to add other categories to the three listed, such as, "If this attitude were a movie star, which movie star would it be?" These also could be used as symbols.

Metaphors can also be considered figures of speech. Metaphors can be used in a variety of capacities in clinical practice. The connection between internal and external reality can be facilitated through the use of metaphors — for example, "My life is a roller coaster." Zuniga (1990) discussed the use of metaphors with Latino clients. Illustrating culturally sensitive practice, "dichos" or sayings from the Latino cultures were used to reframe problems, break resistance, and enhance the therapeutic relationship.

Rituals

Drawing from anthropology and sociology, it can be noted that the power of rituals has long been established. Combs and Freedman (1990, p. 208) stated that ceremonies, a form of ritual, "serve two purposes — to validate an occurrence and to promote change." Rituals, for example, are helpful with endings (e.g., death, divorce) by allowing a person to recognize the past, let go, and move on. Rituals have been used in a variety of therapeutic capacities to meet the unique needs and backgrounds of clients (Imber-Black et al., 1988). Some examples of rituals include holiday activities such as writing Christmas cards, death rituals such as giving a eulogy, and writing — and then burning — a letter to someone unavailable regarding unfinished business.

Storytelling

Storytelling can be used in a variety of therapeutic capacities, as clients can both create and listen to stories that may be based on fantasy or reality. Erickson's clinical use of storytelling with hypnotic trance is well known (Erickson and Rossi, 1980). Storytelling, however, has also been used in more direct ways with individuals. Ucko (1991) discussed the use of folk stories in helping battered women disclose their experience and receive support. Costantino and Malgady (1986) found that "cuento" therapy, the use of folktales, was helpful in reaching high-risk Hispanic children.

White and Epston (1990), in using narrative methods, discussed the "storying of experiences" and the therapeutic aspects of externalizing their problems. Johnson (1991) noted the effect of storytelling on the teller with respect to the resolution of conflict. Stories are central to our functioning. We create stories about all of our experiences, such as those regarding work, family, and recreation.

Brief case illustrations

John, a 34-year-old longshoreman with a ninth-grade education, was married with four children. He was referred through the court system for treatment of his alcoholism. John was tense and spoke little except to voice resentment about "forced treatment". Poetry was introduced in the second session by asking him to write about a time and place he feels most relaxed about. John wrote: "Imagine yourself on the deck of a ship/looking at the bay/on a warm August night/when the sea is peaceful. ..." This poem provided the means for the patient to talk about his work environment, revealing later his drinking pattern at work, where he felt peer pressure. The line starting with "Imagine yourself..." provided an opening for the therapist to begin to enter this client's "life space" (Mazza, 1979).

Claudette was a young single woman dealing with the loneliness of moving to a new geographic region. The poem "The World Is Not a Pleasant Place to Be" (Giovanni, 1972) was used to help her identify feelings associated with loss and to elicit her view of the world. She responded to the lines relating to the unpleasantness of being without someone to love and subsequently reported regret in ending a 2-year relationship with a man. Claudette also felt sad in leaving her physically ill parents. By recognizing the interpersonal aspects of her depression, goals were directed toward increasing activities and establishing ways for her to maintain healthy contact with her parents (e.g., telephone calls, letters, planned visits). In a subsequent session, a tape of Whitney Houston's performance of "The Greatest Love of All" (Creed and Masser, 1977) was used to increase the client's self-esteem and to provide measures of both introspection and support (Mazza, 1988).

Jane was a 33-year-old woman suffering from anxiety due to pressures stemming from her marriage, two small children, career, and home. The poem "Can't Do It All" (Josefowitz, 1983) was used to help the client make an emotional identification with the ambivalence of trying to be a "superwoman". She identified with the lines relating to the dilemma of facing multiple tasks and demands. She took strength from the closing lines, which suggested everything does not have to be done "well". Subsequently, the client was able to let go of some perfectionist tendencies and value her identity while not being compelled to prove herself in each endeavor. The element of choice in her life was developed and later supported with the use of Robert Frost's "The Road Not Taken" (Mazza, 1988).

Poetry therapy and brief treatment*

Brief psychotherapy has an extensive history with increasing attention toward the planned aspect of assessment and intervention (Budman, 1981; Reich and Neenan, 1986; Reid, 1978; Wells, 1994). Mazza (1987a) reported that poetic techniques were suitable for cognitive, affective, and behavioral strategies involved in an eclectic, brief psychotherapy

---

* An earlier version of this section was published by Human Sciences Press in the *Journal of Poetry Therapy*, 2(1), 1988.

model. The role of the poetic in brief treatment will be examined with respect to the following technical characteristics common to various forms of brief psychotherapy: limited time, prompt intervention, limited goals, maintenance of focus, and high therapist activity (Koss et al., 1986). The use of poetry in therapy will include expressive (creating poetry), receptive (reading, listening), and metaphoric modes.

The underlying assumption is that all types of psychotherapy utilize some form of persuasion (Frank, 1973). Winkelman and Saul (1974) attributed the return to the use of suggestion in the human services professions to the development of community mental health centers and brief therapies. The utilization of language and other symbolic means to effect change in the attitude and behavior of the client is part of the poetic approach to practice. Indeed, language is the tool that can help people form relationships. Expression and communication are the aspects of poetry that will be emphasized as an influencing process within and beyond therapy.

Technical characteristics

Recognizing the convergence of many of the brief psychotherapies, the use of the poetic will be examined with respect to the common technical characteristics identified by Koss, Butcher, and Strupp (1986).

Time

In brief psychotherapy, a consideration of both the quantitative (objective) and qualitative (subjective) aspects of time as they relate to therapeutic process and outcome is essential. Alissi and Casper (1985) note the importance of personalized meanings involved in subjective time, particularly as they relate to cultural orientation. From a clinical perspective, adult or "real" time can be distinguished from child or "endless" time (Mann and Goldman, 1982). Germain (1976, p. 420) stated that time "refers to pacing, duration, and rhythm. Time is the silent language that speaks of potentiality and limits, of creativity and death, of change and permanence." Feelings and language are essential components in both therapy and poetry (Crootof, 1969). Poetry can be utilized to elicit here-and-now reactions while extending both backward and forward in time. Dynamic connections between past and present can be developed through time and poetry. Mann and Goldman (1982) discuss time as a personal integrative device that links past, present, and future. Poetry can be particularly helpful in dealing with the affective aspects of time.

The popular song "Memory" (Webber et al., 1982), an adaptation of portions of T.S. Eliot's (1936) "Preludes", lends support to Masserman's (1986) thesis that poetry is music. The power of the poetic to explore the affects of time can be noted in the following:

- *Past:* Lines that recall the beauty and happiness of earlier days
- *Present:* Lines from Eliot's "Preludes" that convey an image of emptiness and despair
- *Future:* Lines relating to a plea for a reconnection to a lost love and affirm the power of touch to bring hope

The song "Memory" and poem "Preludes" can be incorporated within three of the major models of poetry therapy. They are consistent with Leedy's (1969c) prescriptive approach, which utilizes the principle of matching poem to client mood while instilling hope at the end. This is communicated on both sound and lyrical levels. It could also be utilized with Lerner's (1975, 1976, 1982) interpersonal model, in which the poem serves as a vehicle for communication. Schloss' (1976) psychopoetic model might incorporate the poem/song in therapy for the purpose of dramatic enactment. As Mann (1981, p. 27) noted: "Memories are intimately related to important people in our lives and cannot be separated from time in its meaning to us." In identifying life themes, providing clarification and perspective, the poetic has promise. Schloss and Grundy (1978) described particular time techniques that utilize imagery, the senses, and favorite objects from childhood in order to explore memories and identify past hopes and dreams.

Prompt intervention

The use of preexisting poems for the purpose of promoting verbalizations is often nonthreatening. Clients are invited to share their reactions to the poem as a whole or to a particular line or image. While ostensibly talking about a poem, inevitably the client reveals aspects of self. The external object provides a degree of security to the client. Poetry therapy, therefore, can promote early engagement of the client in the therapeutic process by breaking through client resistance while offering an element of control to the client by means of her or his interpretation of the poem.

Wells' (1994) pluralistic (eclectic) short-term treatment model includes five essential goals for the initial interview:

1. Instillation of hope
2. Empathic understanding
3. Identification of one or two major current problems in living
4. Establishing a contract
5. Setting a time limit and giving an initial task

A poem such as Frost's (1915/1964) "The Road Not Taken" exemplifies the interrelationship of the above goals. The poem can elicit the ambivalence associated with difficult decision making (empathy). It can also provide a vehicle to help clarify the problem with subsequent implications for each choice (identification of problem). The poem can also instill hope by suggesting others have had a similar problem (i.e., universalization). Based on the poetic process, a contract to work on the specified problem within a limited time could be established (e.g., career decision, relationship decision). The initial task could be working on a personal diary/log. The degree of specificity would be related to the client problem and therapeutic purpose.

Giving permission to clients to express their feelings offers another element of hope. A poem provides rapid access to both cognitive and affective domains. While problems may not be immediately resolved, hope is embedded through understanding and willingness to make changes. Popular songs might provide rapid access to a client's own psychosocial context. This is especially true with adolescents (Mazza, 1981a).

Poetry writing can also be a very helpful therapeutic tool in providing a vehicle for individuals to express themselves and gain control over fragmented thoughts or feelings. By beginning to write down personal feelings, the individual begins to identify those feelings in a more coherent fashion, thereby promoting a sense of control.

Limited goals

Because goals are limited in brief therapy (e.g., increase ability to cope with a specific problem, reduce depression), a problem-solving perspective could be integrated within therapy through the poetic. For example, with clients suffering from loss such as the death of a loved one, Alice Walker's (1979) "Goodnight Willie Lee, I'll See You in the Morning" could be helpful in identifying feelings associated with loss. The client's current view of the world (such as being alone in a room at home) could also be explored. In recognizing the interpersonal aspects of depression, goals might be directed toward increasing activities and reducing social isolation. An identification of what it would take for the client to smile might also be pursued. The problem-solving perspective would be in terms of identifying and acting on new behaviors outside the therapy session. If the client's personal goal is to develop self-confidence, then a song such as "I Got a Name" (Fox and Gimble, 1973), as performed by Jim Croce, could be utilized to promote introspection and support. Poetry writing can also be utilized in the identification and pursuit of limited goals. Asking clients to complete sentence stems — such as, "I would like to…" or "I keep on because…" or "Life would be better if…" — can also prompt clients toward the development of limited goals.

Maintenance of focus

Focus in the therapy sessions could be increased through the use of a preexisting poem by directing attention to a particular line or asking individuals how they might change the poem to reflect their thoughts or feelings more accurately. When there is a drifting away from a central issue by an individual, the use of a poem can focus the session and reassess the purpose of therapy. For example, some lines from Shakespeare's play *Macbeth* (Act IV, Scene III) can be introduced:

> *Give sorrow words: the grief that does not*
> *Speak*
> *Whispers the o'er-fraught heart and bids it*
> *Break*

The poetic lines can provide the opportunity for individuals to focus on the issue of loss and pursue the necessary grief work.

High therapist activity

The aforementioned activities and goals require a significant amount of therapist activity, particularly with respect to the preselection and incorporation of poetry within the therapeutic context. However, flexibility in application and a willingness to suspend the use of any poetic technique are requisites for effective therapy.

Comment

The use of poetry in brief therapy can serve as a therapeutic agent in promoting client change. Poetic techniques seem to be compatible with the technical aspects of brief therapy; however, empirical validation has not been provided. Poetic techniques do not work in all situations. In fact, the use of poetry can hinder the therapeutic process by promoting intellectualizations, focusing on a therapist's agenda rather than a client's needs, or evoking feelings that clients may not be ready to deal with in their current state.

Poetics in the stages of brief therapy*

The following case example will illustrate the use of poetic techniques throughout Wolberg's (1965) stages of an eclectic brief psychotherapy model. *Jenny*, a 26-year-old, single, Caucasian woman with a presenting problem of "feeling nervous and overwhelmed", was seen at a private counseling agency. The client had submitted her resignation from her job as an administrative assistant. She was scheduled to move across the country for a better position in her profession. Treatment planning was therefore externally limited to 8 weeks.

---

* An earlier version of this section was published by Brunner/Mazel in *The American Journal of Social Psychiatry*, 7(2), 1987.

Supportive phase (sessions 1 and 2)

Jenny was tense, anxious, and tearful in the early part of the first interview. She indicated a nomadic pattern of moving and described herself as a "short-termer". She had gone through a series of job changes, geographical moves, and relationships with men. Jenny experienced moderate depression in looking backward at perceived failures and missed opportunities. She experienced anxiety in looking at potential failures and lack of acceptance. The poetic was utilized to deal with Jenny's feelings of helplessness and anxiety. She reported that she was a runner and had made a commitment to run her first marathon in 6 weeks. Although Jenny was engaged in the appropriate training, she was fearful and considering dropping out. Running and the race became the metaphor for her life and for the psychotherapeutic process. Intricately related to running the race were Jenny's concerns with identity, performance, and closure. Discussion about her preparation for the race and the many aspects of her move to a new city became a parallel endeavor.

Running was essentially utilized on both concrete and symbolic levels. On the concrete level, she had the opportunity to achieve mastery over a challenge by completing the race. This would also improve her self-esteem and instill hope. She also had to deal with special tasks involved in training. On a symbolic level, the race represented risks that she experienced in other aspects of her life (e.g., intimate relationships, confronting family members, assuming authority in career positions). In the past, Jenny's approach to risk was to move on and to run the "short races" that she was sure to complete. This time she was pursuing a distance challenge on many levels. Jenny was also doing something she preferred and enjoyed rather then feeling compelled to please others. This relates perhaps to a poetic philosophy in life that could emerge by tapping her feelings in a struggle to create something uniquely her own. By discussing the poetry in herself, she could begin to connect to others.

Expression of emotion was a significant factor in the early stages of treatment. Jenny was initially very apologetic for crying in the first interview. The popular song "Don't Cry Out Loud" (Allen and Bayer-Sager, 1976), as performed by Melissa Manchester, was played during the second session. The song includes the lines that pertain to a lesson learned early in life about the importance of keeping feelings out of sight. The emotional identification with the song prompted a cathartic response from Jenny as she related that crying meant failure and that she often disappointed her parents.

The poetic approaches (metaphor and poem/song) were helpful in identifying problem and target areas for intervention (developmental and transitional issues involved with relocating) and conveying empathic understanding (connecting to the importance of running, linking with the pain involved in holding back one's feelings). The above factors contribute to instilling hope, which is further supported by establishing weekly contacts and noting that there will be an end to therapy. The message is that the problems are "treatable" within a limited period of time. In this way, time becomes an independent variable in treatment that will also be considered in the separation-individuation process. Jenny agreed to train for the marathon and prepare for her relocation while examining her personal and family concerns. Jenny's initial task was to write her thoughts and feelings daily in a personal journal.

Apperceptive phase (sessions 3 and 4)

This stage involves the client's development of insight regarding specified problems. Therapist interpretation and clarification are directed toward identifying how past problems affect personality structure and relate to current problems. This relates to the affective aspects of time. The poem "Brooding" by David Ignatow (1964) was utilized in the third session. It includes lines that relate to the issue of "being good enough". Jenny was able to relate the family, social, and personal issues, which evolved into a life theme for her: "You have succeeded in getting yourself to be different; nevertheless, you continue to feel that you are and always have been inferior and inadequate, a loser" (Mann, 1981, p. 36). Some attention was directed in therapy toward how Jenny developed and maintained that theme. This included cognitive distortions and interpersonal behaviors that prevented her from discovering a very special part of herself.

In an effort to crystallize the identity issue and instill hope, the song "I Got a Name" (Fox and Gimble, 1973) was played. It includes lines relating to maintaining one's identity and dreams through difficult times. Jenny's reaction was immediate and insightful. She recognized her need for external validation; however, whenever the possibilities arose, she fled (fearing rejection). She recognized her "highways" (an image used in the song) and the consequences of loneliness.

Action phase (sessions 5 and 6)

On concrete and metaphoric levels, the long-distance race was broken down into manageable parts. Jenny decided to run a 10-kilometer (6.2-mile) race as a preparatory exercise. After successful completion of the race, Jenny adopted "Lady, Lady, Lady" as her own song (Forsey, 1983). The song includes lines relating to fear about not reaching a dream, maintaining a protective mask, hearing that there is someone out there wanting to touch her, and pursuing her dream "running like the wind". This became a theme song for Jenny which she carried with her through the marathon (26.2 miles). To Jenny, the song was an affirmation of her femininity, strength, identity, and desire for intimacy. She did not have to be alone. Choices were being restored. Subsequently, Jenny chose to speak directly to friends whom she was having difficulty leaving.

Another aspect of the action phase was Jenny's willingness to maintain a personal journal, which served to restore control to her over some difficult areas and provided an additional means for self-expression. After identifying several concerns about her new job, she made telephone calls and received adequate clarification. Jenny also decided to visit her parents (approximately 100 miles away) and, while not resolving all conflicts, was able to speak in a positive way about herself. She informed her parents that she was moving (about 2000 miles away) and received a moderate degree of support.

Integrative phase (sessions 7 and 8)

In this termination stage of therapy, Jenny was able to consolidate some of her therapeutic gain while recognizing there was still more to do beyond therapy (or in another therapeutic context, should the need arise). Jenny did successfully complete the marathon. She also completed all tasks regarding the preparation for relocation. As part of the anticipatory planning process, the poem "If I Should Cast Off This Tattered Coat" by Stephen Crane (1895/1970) was utilized to deal with the unknown future. Questions regarding how Jenny would deal with loss, frustration, and success in the future were asked. Jenny recognized that indeed there would be mistakes and disappointments but that she could "feel bad" and press on. The poem "Can't Do It All" (Josefowitz, 1983) was shared to lend further support. This poem also dealt with an emerging life philosophy that recognized sensitivity and choice as strengths.

Finally the issue of separation in therapy was addressed, in part, through the song "Goodbye" (Watson and Blades, 1985), as recorded by Night Ranger. It includes lines relating to the vicissitudes of life and difficulty in saying goodbye. This song was helpful in tracing and acknowledging Jenny's development through therapy. Although it was still hard to say goodbye (for both therapist and client), Jenny was able to hear it, say it, and pass through the transition. John Denver's (1975) song "Looking for Space", with lines relating to the many unanswered questions in life's journey, provided a perspective of acceptance. Jenny's positive response to the words relating to inner peace and hope provided an evaluation of her success in therapy and an element of hope that she will complete her own poem.

Comment

Inevitably, all therapy, like poetry, remains unfinished. In keeping with Kanfer's (1979) notion of an instigative approach to therapy, the poetic techniques and process serve to promote change outside of the therapy sessions. Although strategies sometimes overlap in various phases, it appears that the poetic is consistent with the essential flow from affective to cognitive to behavioral and finally to integrative states in Wolberg's (1965) short-term therapy model.

The use of poetry in brief therapy can be helpful in providing the client with new experiences that promote early engagement in the therapeutic process. Poetic approaches are suitable for cognitive strategies, such as clarification and focusing; affective strategies, such as expression of feeling (catharsis) and relationship building; and behavioral strategies, such as the use of specified activities and contracting. Poetry, music, and time have a unique interrelationship in the therapeutic process that can span a wide range of client concerns. The poetic has the promise of combining ego-supportive with problem-solving approaches. This may, in fact, be one contribution toward the understanding of the convergence of a number of theoretical foundations involved in brief therapy.

chapter three

Poetry therapy and family psychology*

The application of the poetry therapy practice model explored in Chapter two focused on individual therapy. The three major components (receptive/prescriptive, expressive/creative, and symbolic/ceremonial) also apply to family and group therapy. The focus of this chapter will be on the explanation and application of poetry therapy techniques appropriate for family psychology. This includes working with individuals on family issues, working with the family unit, and dealing with couple/family issues in group treatment.

The clinical use of metaphor, narrative, storytelling, journal writing, song lyrics, poetry, and related language arts in family therapy has received increased attention in the professional literature (Mazza, 1996). In a time of transition and transformation for the American family, poetry therapy can serve as the interlocking element for a multitude of family therapy approaches sensitive to culture, different value systems, gender, and developmental issues.

The practice of systemic, constructivist, strategic, structural, intergenerational, and symbolic-experiential family therapies incorporates poetic elements. For example, in constructivist therapy there is an emphasis on narrative; in structural and strategic therapy there is considerable use of reframing; and the use of metaphor can be found in all of the above approaches.

---

* An earlier version of this chapter was published by Haworth in the *Journal of Family Social Work*, 1(3), 1996.

Receptive/prescriptive

Traditional bibliotherapy

The use of traditional bibliotherapy or what Hynes and Hynes-Berry (1986) refer to as "reading bibliotherapy" can be useful in family practice as a means to provide guidance. Reading is generally assigned to the client, and it may be something direct, such as a book on parenting skills, or something indirect, such as a story on relationships. Cohen (1993) also noted the use of literature on a self-help basis. Lerner and Mahlendorf's (1991) *Life Guidance Through Literature* includes a review and analysis of literary works relating to critical issues and problems throughout the life cycle. Pardeck and Pardeck (1987) discussed the use of bibliotherapy by school social workers with children experiencing difficulties with changing family forms.

Introducing literature (particularly poetry) and song lyrics

As noted earlier, this technique involves the selection and reading of a poem or other piece of literature for use in therapy. With a clear purpose in mind (e.g., validate feelings, promote self-disclosure, facilitate interaction, universalize an experience), the clinician can introduce the poem to the client by connecting it to the content or dialogue of the session. The poem can be helpful in breaking resistance because it provides the client with a safe distance for making an emotional identification. By ostensibly talking about a poem, the client begins to talk about self. In essence, the poem serves as a springboard for him or her to disclose feelings, goals, and values. Questions about the poem should be directed toward the client's perception (e.g., "What does it mean to you? Is there a particular line or stanza that you could connect with or call your own? Is there anything that you would like to change or modify in this poem?"). The use of song lyrics and an accompanying audiotape can also be incorporated in this technique (Ho and Settles, 1984; Hodas, 1991; Mazza, 1979, 1988a, 1993). Table 1 (Mazza, 1999) identifies some poems and songs that have been particularly useful in family therapy.

Expressive/creative

Family collaborative poem

Family members are invited to contribute one or more lines to a family poem on a topic relating to the theme or mood of the session. The family poems are often typed, and copies are given to each member of the family in the following session (Mazza, 1979, 1988a, 1993). The poem can serve to validate feelings, empower clients, facilitate interaction, and promote discussion of family issues.

Table 1a Table of Poems

Theme	Title	Poet	Source
Anxiety/risk	"If I Should Cast..."	Stephen Crane	Dore[a]
Family/strengths	"Nikki Rosa"	Nikki Giovanni	Gillan and Gillan[b]/ Sewell[c]
Grief	"Good Night, Willie Lee..."	Alice Walker	Sewell[c]
Anger	"A Just Anger"	Marge Piercy	Sewell[c]
Alienation	"Alone/December Night"	Victor Cruz	Dore[a]
Communication	"Two Friends"	David Ignatow	Dore[a]
Intergenerational issues	"Legacies"	Nikki Giovanni	Gillan and Gillan[b]
Community	"In the Inner City"	Lucille Clifton	Gillan and Gillan[b]
Alcoholism	"My Papa's Waltz"	Theodore Roethke	Dore[a]
Dreams/hopes deferred	"Harlem"	Langston Hughes	Dore[a]

Table 1b Discography

Theme	Song	Performing artist
Parent/child	"Cat's in the Cradle"	Harry Chapin
	"Ugly Kid Joe"	Ricky Skaggs
Alcoholism	"Little Rock"	Collin Raye
AIDS; father/son	"Last Song"	Elton John
Parent/child separation	"Letting Go"	Suzy Bogguss
Life cycle (mother/daughter)	"How Can I Help You Say Goodbye?"	Patty Loveless
Infidelity	"All These Years"	Sawyer Brown
Death of a child	"Tears in Heaven"	Eric Clapton
Fathers/daughters	"If I Could"	Ray Charles
Love/commitment	"What's Forever For?"	Michael Martin Murphy
Relationships/distance	"Get Here"	Oleta Adams

[a] Dore, A., Ed. (1970) *The Premier Book of Major Poets*, Greenwich, CT: Fawcett (a general anthology of poetry).

[b] Gillan, M.A. and Gillan, J., Eds. (1994) *Unsettling America: An Anthology of Contemporary Multicultural Poetry*, New York: Penguin.

[c] Sewell, M., Ed. (1991) *Cries of the Spirit: A Celebration of Women's Spirituality*, Boston: Beacon (a sourcebook of poetry and phrase including sections on intimacy, mothering, generations, death and loss, and re-mything).

Source: Adapted from Mazza, N. (1999) The poetic in family social work, *Journal of Family Social Work*, in press. With permission.

The following is an example of a collaborative poem that was used early in therapy:

I'm most happy at home	[clinician]
When my feelings are respected	[14-year-old daughter]
When my family listens to me	[17-year-old son]
When we do things together	[40-year-old father]
When we are together	[39-year-old mother]

The parents' presenting problem was "family bickering and general dissatisfaction". By collectively stating what was important to the family, the members were subsequently able to specify how and when the above elements in the poem could be achieved. Each member also took responsibility for contributing to a happier family.

In a group relating to family issues, the collaborative poem can serve to universalize and validate feelings, advance cohesion, and provide an element of control to the members (Mazza and Prescott, 1981; Mazza and Price, 1985). The following is an excerpt from a poem on divorce written by a fourth- and fifth-grade, school-based children's group (Horowitz et al., 1987, pp.61–62):

I'm confused sometimes
With whom I love better.
Sometimes I get mad at my Dad.
Sometimes I get mad at my Mom.
Sometimes I get sick of both of them. ...
Sometimes I punch my pillow.
I like to get my feelings out. ...
I get on my bed and lay
Until the end of the day,
And think how my life will
Be in some very other way.

Family poems: borrowed, brief, rational, and extended

Gladding (1985) developed the following series of structured poetic exercises.

Borrowed family poems
Borrowing from a familiar source, such as a song or movie, each family member is invited to express in one or two lines what he or she perceives as the family's current level of functioning.

Brief family poems
Similar to the borrowed family poems, this exercise allows family members to describe their feelings about themselves as individuals and

their family as a whole. Sentence stems are offered to help facilitate this process. For example (Gladding, 1985, p. 240): "Our family is a ... [name a type of house, such as brick, dilapidated]" or "I feel like a ... [name an animal form]."

Rational family poems

Building on the "shoulds, musts, and oughts" that family members express in describing how their family works, each member is asked to write a poem with two rhyming lines. For example (Gladding, 1985, p. 241): "My son is a jerk/He should keep his room straight/Every night he should be in by eight." Toward the end of therapy, family members are again asked to write a poem on the same subject written about earlier in the treatment. A measure of success can be found if irrational thinking does not appear in this poem.

Extended family poems

Members are asked to make up four lists of words. The first list describes the physical make-up of the family (e.g., single parent, three members, all male). The second list contains common features (e.g., color of hair, sensitivity, determination). The third list includes activities that the family members enjoy together (e.g., reading, camping, church). The fourth list contains words that others would use to describe the family (e.g., close, busy, quiet). A poem is constructed from these lists.

Dyadic poem

A couple is asked to develop a two-line poem (each person contributing one line) about the meaning of a song or poem that was presented to them. The introduction of a poem or song to stimulate the writing exercise is optional, though, as the couple can simply be instructed to write a two-line poem about their relationship. The following poem (Mazza and Prescott, 1981, p. 56) was written by a couple married 6 years and dealing with career and self-fulfillment issues: "Free, free, free never there/Was it all worthwhile?" This technique can also be useful in assessment (Mazza, 1993, p. 53): (1) Were the lines complementary or contrasting? (2) Who went first? (3) How was the task approached by the couple?

Sentence stems/completion

The sentence stem provides a form of moderate prestructuring to facilitate self-expression. Koch (1970) offers a number of techniques to encourage creative writing among children. Examples include writing a poem in which every line begins with "I wish..." or using contrasting themes by alternating lines ("I used to be.../But now I..."). Following is an example of dealing with a communication problem between a mother and her 12-year-old son:

Son:
I used to be angry
But now I control my temper.

Mother:
I used to be confused about John
But now I understand.

The above example served to help open up the discussion regarding grief (death of the father/husband), anger, and related family issues.

Gumina (1980) proposed the use of a series of sentence-completion tasks as an ancillary technique in sex therapy. Partners take turns responding. For example (p. 203):

Tom:
If I weren't so angry … I might listen to you.

Joan:
If I weren't so angry … I wouldn't pressure you.

The technique can of course be used in family therapy to help promote communication and insight.

Family time

This exercise is an acrostic using the word "family" — each line of the poem begins with a letter from the word. The exercise could begin by asking a family member to make a list of things or behaviors that describe his or her family. The poems can later be shared among family members to promote discussion and perhaps serve as an impetus to plan a family activity (Pickerill, 1993). The following was written by a 13-year-old girl whose parents are divorced and have joint custody of her:

Father, who loves and helps me with life.
And who helps me believe in myself.
Mother, who cares for me even
If she's not there.
Lots of love is in my houses even when
Yelling or we're sleeping.

Sensory poem

This prestructured poetic exercise developed from *Ghostwriter…* (1993) involves the identification of a topic or feeling and subsequent development of a poem using the senses. The following is an example written by a 10-year-old boy:

Family is the color red.
It sounds like chimes.
It feels like love.
It tastes like pizza.
It smells like brownies.
It makes me feel like shouting.

Letter writing

A number of approaches involve the use of letter writing in therapy. Nunnally and Lipchick (1990) noted the use of letters written by the therapist after his or her session which are then read to the clients before they exit. The technique is discussed in the brief solution-focused model advanced by deShazer. Sometimes the letters are constructed with a team who had been behind the one-way mirror, and sometimes the letters are mailed to the family members. A client can also be encouraged to write a letter to a deceased family member or members unavailable due to divorce. For example, in the case of divorce, a child might write a letter to a parent who has exhibited avoidance behavior. The child might also write a letter out of fear of "not being able to say what I want to say because I'll get scared and confused." Letter writing is a useful method of working through anger, frustration, and/or the grief process related to a number of life circumstances. In cases of divorce, the letter can sometimes serve as a catalyst for healthy dialogue between parent and child. Sloman and Pipitone (1991) provided guidelines for parents to write letters to their children when there are problems in communication.

White and Epston (1990) write letters to family members as a way to help clients externalize problems, break resistance, and re-story their experience:

- Letters of invitation invite missing family members to join a session.
- Redundancy letters are designed to get family members to give up an inappropriate role by showing it is no longer necessary.
- Letters of prediction are used as a follow-up device which can also function as a measure of support for healthy behavior.

Counterreferral letters, letters of reference, letters for special occasions, brief letters, and letters as a narrative are other variations of the use of letters in therapeutic capacities.

Programmed writing

L'Abate and Cox (1992) proposed the use of workbooks and specific lesson plans regarding a particular problem to be given as an outside assignment and later discussed in therapy. L'Abate (1993) provided a description of this technique used with a family having arguments. The specific lesson plans given during sessions were as follows:

1. Lesson requiring family members to describe independently (on a detailed form) their arguments and then setting a time to discuss them as a family
2. Lesson involving an explanation of the function of the problem and reframing
3. Lesson prescribing arguments
4. Lesson on recording and reading the arguments
5. Lesson on how to deal with the most pressing pattern
6. Lesson on how to deal with the pattern occurring with the second highest frequency

Symbolic/ceremonial

Rituals

Rituals play a significant role in working with families. For example, the development of new customs and traditions for newly formed single-parent and stepfamilies can be helpful in promoting a healthy transition. Rituals have been used in a variety of ways in family therapy to meet the unique needs and backgrounds of families (Imber-Black et al., 1988). Some examples of rituals include a prayer at family dinner; death rituals, such as a special ceremony and burial when a pet has died; and special celebrations to recognize a success.

Storytelling

Storytelling can be used in a number of ways with families. Whitaker (1992) examines the use of stories and fairy tales in healing the mother/ daughter relationship. Chavis (1987a) presents a collection of short stories depicting family relationships and stages of development. Friedman (1990) offers 24 fables of animals that can serve as an excellent resource for dealing with family relationships. Stories can also be found in popular music — for example, Harry Chapin's performance of "Cat's in the Cradle" (Chapin and Chapin, 1974). In their discussion of Keen's audiotape on "Telling Your Story", Becvar and Becvar (1993) noted that one of the problems involved in divorce is losing the person with whom one has shared a story. In essence, each family member carries and creates stories.

Metaphors

Metaphors can be used in a variety of capacities in family practice. As noted in individual therapy, a connection between internal and external reality can be facilitated through the use of metaphors — for example, "this family is a sinking ship" or "this family is a boiler about to blow" or reference to a "family dance". Cornille and Inger (1992), noting the often defensive posture of couples and families in therapy, described the use of the "armor metaphor" as a therapeutic intervention to promote open communication. Gatz and Christie (1991) discussed the use of metaphor in marital group therapy with respect to the stages of group development.

Brief illustrations

When the M. family, consisting of a 55-year-old alcoholic father, a 52-year-old mother, and four children (ages 17, 14, 13, and 10), began therapy, the father refused to come to the early sessions. The family was asked to construct a collaborative poem describing what it was like at home on a usual evening:

When I'm home...	[therapist]
I try to understand everything	[Mrs. M.]
I feel like moving	[Kathy, 17]
Or going out	[Carol, 14]
Or watching television	[Ron, 13]
Or going back to the back room	[Scott, 10]

This poem provided the basis for family discussion and revealed a mother overwhelmed and overinvolved, while the children were all trying to pull away. Afraid to mention their fears and pain individually, the family members were able to voice their despair collectively. In an attempt to validate and perhaps universalize some of their feelings, Theodore Roethke's poem, "My Papa's Waltz" (1942/ 1970), which describes a child's experience with an alcoholic father, was read to this family. The complexity of the problem was demonstrated, and subsequently each family member began to identify personal needs. "My Papa's Waltz" provided a means of interaction and helped to engage the family in treatment. Subsequently, the father came in for treatment (Mazza, 1979).

During group therapy with wives of alcoholics who ranged in age from 25 to 52, both popular music and poetry were used. One of the songs played was Barry Manilow's "Sandra" (Manilow and Anderson, 1974), a song that includes lines relating to unfulfilled wishes and the despair about never taking time for one's self. The group members recognized that their descriptions of Sandra's feelings of frustration, emptiness, and loneliness pertained to themselves. This theme was further expressed in a poem written by the group:

Frustration
Frustration is having someone not understand me...
What is hurt?
Feeling rejected.
Hating myself.
The things I can't do anything about
My husband's drinking
Other people's actions
Family, children
They aggravate you.
And we come full circle.

In this poem, each woman was able to define for herself the stresses of living in a household with an alcoholic husband. In writing this poem, the women in the group seemed to examine their own feelings and to deal with themselves and each other honestly. They began to recognize their frailties and self-imposed limitations. The cyclical nature of the problem was demonstrated in the closing line. The poem provides both insight and hope — the hope lies in the women's ability to begin to verbalize their problems and in their willingness to respond to each other (Mazza, 1979).

Couples group[*]

Poetry was utilized as a medium in a short-term couples enrichment group conducted at a university counseling center (Mazza and Prescott, 1981). The group was designed to help couples who were committed to development of a relationship or rediscovering ways to make the relationship more rewarding. The goals included the promotion of individual as well as couple growth. The group consisted of fairly articulate members, ranging in education from some college experience to advanced degrees. The four couples had a mean age of 25 years. Two couples were married, and two couples had lived together for over a year. None of the members had received any previous counseling or mental health services. The group was co-led by one male and one female therapist.

First session

The primary theme of the opening session was space in relationships. The therapists had planned to use the lyrics of John Denver's (1975) song "Looking for Space" to introduce the theme and facilitate discussion; however, in a number of disparate ways, the group was already

---

* An earlier version of this section was published by Brunner/Mazel in *The American Journal of Family Therapy*, 9(1), 1981.

dealing with this issue. It was later that the poem/song proved to be helpful in connecting the individual expressions and providing closure for the session.

Third session

One couple brought in the lyrics and tape of the Carole King (1972) song "Bitter With the Sweet" to share with the group. The couple had been married for 5 years and was experiencing the strain of dual career demands. The lines especially important to them related to the demands on one's time. The lines struck a common chord with the entire group. Later, they all seemed to agree that taking time and space for themselves was all right. Some members began to recognize and/or accept that there are both bitter and sweet aspects of relationships.

The theme emerging from the discussion and interaction centered on trying to feel complete. This became the title of the group's joint effort toward a collaborative poem:

> *Trying to feel complete*
> *I sometimes lose the balance*
> *And fall down on my head.*
> *I get very stiff*
> *A cardboard face*
> *Tight inside*
> *Like a shell that I want to break out of*
> *But I prevent myself from doing so*
> *And feel self-destructive.*
> *Imagining dread consequences*
> *That do not have to be.*
> *A cocoon and never a butterfly.*
> *Yes I can fly*
> *But I have to break out*
> *Then I'll be complete.*

In the first line of this poem, individuals spoke of the balance in their relationships. After the poem was completed, the therapists asked the following types of questions: What happens when you fall down? Could you tell me more about the shell? Cocoon? Butterfly? How do you manage to stay in the shell? One member had taken responsibility for remaining closed or in the shell with the line, "But I prevent myself from doing so." The implications for the relationship were discussed. It was also pointed out by the group that the "dread consequences" were a product of the imagination and may be contributing to the "cardboard face".

The poem ends with hope ("Yes I can fly") and a task ("But I have to break out"). Individually and collectively, members had begun to think in terms of specific things they would like to do to improve their lives and relationships.

The poem was read by a group member, which provided further cohesion and validation. The therapist asked the group members if the poem was indicative of what they were feeling. All members responded positively. The group was able to provide images and metaphors that served as vehicles for self-disclosure. The collaborative poem was later typed and distributed to group members in the following session.

Fourth session

Stephen Crane's (1895/1970) poem "If I Should Cast Off This Tattered Coat" was shared with the group by the therapists. The purpose was to deal with the risk and anxiety involved in new experiences. For example, questions during the discussion might include, "What happens if I become disillusioned or frustrated?" After the poem was read, the group members were put in dyads with each couple sharing and discussing the poem. They were later brought together and constructed couplets, including the following: "Free, free, free, never there/Was it all worthwhile?" This couplet was written by introspective partners dealing with their pursuit of freedom and careers. In that pursuit, they were losing perspective on their relationship.

The process of writing the dyadic poems (couplets) was particularly helpful in pointing out differences in the ways the partners viewed various issues. Likewise, it often illuminated similarities in their thinking and feeling which served to validate their relationship. This technique was used by couples outside of the sessions on their own initiative.

Sixth (final) session

Simon and Garfunkel's "The Sounds of Silence" (Simon, 1964) was helpful in dealing with many of the unspoken concerns of the group. This selection was helpful in providing the transition to termination issues. One member brought in an excellent closing poem/song by Gilberto Gil (1979) entitled "Here and Now". This member was perceptive in introducing it at the appropriate time. It provided a validation of the group and its relationships. The group members reminded each other of the importance of dealing with the here and now.

Comment

The aforementioned techniques and illustrations require caution. While an example of an enrichment group for couples was presented, there still remains special consideration for intensive couples group therapy. The next chapter will focus on issues unique to poetic approaches in group therapy.

chapter four

Group therapy: advancing process and outcome through poetic methods

Poetry therapy in group treatment has also been used in receptive/prescriptive, expressive/creative, and symbolic/ceremonial modes. Very often the above modes are used in combination with various groups.

Buck and Kramer (1974) noted that the use of poetry therapy facilitates group process. They observed a cumulative effect wherein group members learned the procedures of using poetry in therapy and developed a sensitivity to group functioning. Lauer and Goldfield (1970), in an earlier report, noted this phenomenon with respect to the role of creative writing in group therapy. Lessner (1974) found that the introduction of poetry to group sessions served as a catalyst for advancing group process. Lerner (1982) advanced an interpersonal poetry therapy model for groups. Mazza and Prescott (1981), while working with a couples group (see Chapter three), found support for Buck and Kramer's cumulative effect. Goldstein (1989) reported that poetry therapy was consistent with interpersonal theory and the therapeutic factors in group therapy observed by Yalom (1995).

Diana (1998) discussed the use of storytelling in group treatment with forensic inpatients. Wenz and McWhirter (1990, pp. 39–40) used creative writing as an adjunct to group therapy. The specific exercises described included the development of a personal logo. Group members were instructed to "play with doodles you have always enjoyed drawing, visualize an important aspect of your life, capture a favorite place on Earth; keep playing and drawing until a symbol seems right for you. And then tell a story about it." This exercise, drawing on the power of both expression and symbol, integrated poetry and art.

The use of poetry writing in groups is extensive (e.g., Davis, 1979; Kramer, 1990; Lauer and Goldfield, 1970; Plasse, 1995). Mazza (1979, 1981a, 1981b), Chase (1989), Yochim (1994), and Golden (1994) reported on the collaborative poem in group work. Using a group therapy model that included receptive and expressive (collaborative poem) components, Mazza (1981b) found that poetry therapy advanced group cohesion. Golden (1994) isolated the collaborative poem variable and found that it did advance cohesion in therapy groups.

Application*

The following is an example of the Mazza (1981b) poetry therapy group model combining receptive/prescriptive and expressive/creative modes. The group was for moderately depressed university students. The case (Mazza and Price, 1985) will be examined with respect to specific group developmental stages noted by Garland, Jones, and Kolodny (1965): (1) pre-affiliation, power, and control; (2) intimacy/differentiation; and (3) separation/termination.

The group consisted of six members (two males, four females) ranging in age from 18 to 36. All of the members were undergraduate students. Most of the members had previously enjoyed reading some form of literature and/or listening to music. A 7-week format was chosen by taking into consideration the academic calendar and time limits of the counseling center. Within the time frame of both the semester and the length of group treatment, students would be facing deadlines, making decisions, and completing tasks; therefore, time could be used as a treatment variable consistent with other student responsibilities. Each session lasted 1 to 2 hours. The group was co-led by one male and one female clinician.

Model and techniques

Poetry and/or pop music were used within a group treatment model that combined the selection of preexisting poems or songs and the development of collaborative (group) poems (Mazza, 1981b). The use of preexisting poems (e.g., Stephen Crane's "If I Should Cast Off This Tattered Coat") was primarily based on the isoprinciple of selecting a poem that is close in mood to that of a client (Leedy, 1969c). This principle was extended to include group mood and particular themes that evolved during the treatment. A cassette tape was used for the music technique, and copies of the lyrics and/or poems were provided to the group members.

---

* An earlier version of this section was published by Haworth in *Social Work with Groups*, 8(2), 1985.

The technique of the collaborative poem was generally used toward the end of each session. This involved the creation of a group poem with each member having the opportunity to contribute lines. The group poem was initiated by the group leader(s), who asked for a predominant theme or feeling in the group session. The poems were later typed and copies distributed to group members at the beginning of the next session. By distributing copies of the group's collaborative poem to members in the subsequent session, a time link was established. Members could choose to discuss the poem and/or move on to other areas. This model of poetry therapy is generally incorporated within an eclectic group treatment framework.

First session

The initial group session included introductory issues (e.g., review of time designated for group), definition of group goals, explanation of the format, and a general exploration of member concerns. The commonality of depression was acknowledged by group members through David Ignatow's (1964) poem "Brooding", which includes lines relating to never being "good enough" for friends and family. Members were cautious in speaking, offering minimal self-disclosures. The use of a preexisting poem was helpful in providing some early structure and allowing members to talk about feelings in a nonthreatening manner. In this first session, the poem was helpful in establishing an atmosphere that promoted member participation (discussing and/or creating a poem).

This maximized the use of time available while dealing with personally meaningful issues that may have been of concern for a long time. Time was viewed as hopeless, with individuals being helpless in dealing with family relationships, academic failure, and psychosexual issues. By beginning to identify and define their feelings, group members could perceive time in a more helpful ("I don't have to decide today" or "I reserve the right to change my mind later") and productive ("We completed a poem today") manner. The collaborative poem would also prove helpful in subsequent sessions to signify the end of each session.

The group collaborative poem entitled "Depression" included the following lines:

> *...inside a sinkhole*
> *Dark, grasping*
> *Restless, listless, tired*
> *Don't want to do anything*
> *...feel FAT and ugly*
> *Why would anybody like me?*

This poem reflected a collection of individualized feelings associated with depression. It is consistent with early group development in which members can maintain distance on the one hand, while becoming involved with other members in the commonality of depression.

Second session

Power and control issues emerged during this session. One member (male) arrived late and maintained a posture of silence and noninvolvement. This nonverbal communication served to set the member apart while drawing attention from others attempting to involve him in the group discussion. At approximately the midway point in the session, one of the group leaders introduced Dave Loggins' (1974) "So You Couldn't Get to Me" to the group. This song was consistent with both the theme (isolation) and mood (depression, frustration) of the group.

The timing of the use of the song was geared to tap into the group process and facilitate forward movement. Also, the melody of this song evoked a rather slow and relaxed pace that helped to reduce tension and allowed the group members (one male member, in particular) to express their feelings. The song includes lines relating to the desire to be isolated from a former lover. The silent member identified with the feelings expressed in the song. He began to share some difficult times he had experienced with a woman. Some members joined in supporting him, while another member intellectualized and voiced negative feelings toward males. In fact, the song evoked personal reactions by most of the members.

Group members were asked by one of the leaders: "If you had an island, who would you invite onto it?" A group member was able to establish some independence and raise the important issue of personal space by responding that she would not invite anyone and that the question for her pertained more to deciding for whom she would leave her island in order to visit. This member was able to lessen her dependency on others while establishing the boundaries of the island.

The collaborative poem that day was entitled "Anger". It revealed an attempt to begin an examination of depression; however, there is little cohesion with contrasting lines (e.g., "Throwing stones at the moon/Energy not directed well..."). The collaborative poem was particularly helpful in this session in activating the silent and most visibly depressed member. He was asked to write down the lines for the group. This involved getting out of his chair and recording lines on a flip-chart. The activity appeared to mobilize this member's energy and to heighten his affect as he became more verbal and participated in the creation of the poem.

Third session

When the collaborative poem from the previous week was reviewed, issues pertaining to the expenditure of time and energy were discussed. Particularly, some members were discontent about an apparently disproportionate amount of time being spent on some individuals. Quiet members were able to voice their needs and concerns by initially responding to the collaborative poem. Subsequently, member and leader responsibilities were clarified and the energy redirected. Jim Croce's "I Got a Name" (Fox and Gimble, 1973) provided some impetus and validation for the above expression. The melody of this song helped accelerate the pace of the session. Issues of identity, family and interpersonal relationships, and career options were brought up in the session.

The collaborative poem entitled "Relief" demonstrates the therapeutic value of this session. It also suggests the early development of trust in the group and subsequent challenges.

> **Relief**
> *Is voicing*
> *What you've been afraid to say.*
> *Taking a weight*
> *Off my back*
> *And feeling more free.*
> *Looking*
> *At the feelings that are okay.*
> *Are there any feelings*
> *That are not okay?*
> *Sometimes*
> *I just don't know my feelings*
> *And that's okay, too.*

In effect, the last lines of the poem validated the confusion and struggle while the group continued to develop.

Fourth session

This session involved more risk taking as more meaningful personal experiences were shared (difficulty dealing with a former spouse, parental pressures to attend college, feelings of inadequacy, etc.). Stephen Crane's (1895/1970) poem "If I Should Cast Off This Tattered Coat" was used to help deal with the anxiety involved with risk taking and the unknown. The poem was helpful in dealing with the risk of expressing one's self in the group. One member had been talking about her "writer's block" in completing a term paper. This was later used to connect to a "group block" in which it was difficult to express self. Issues of risk and trust were of central concern. The group responded to the image of the tattered coat, noting for some it was a secure coat. For others, they were ready to "go free into the mighty sky." Discussion included how some individuals were trying to "hold back the clock" to avoid possible rejection or failure. Mention of the group calendar (amount of weeks left in the group) was made by the leaders, and they discussed how this time would be used to deal with the above issues. Essentially, time was both a lever and point of discussion for the group.

Initially, the collaborative poem for this week had no title:

> *Conflicts with each other*
> *Delving into each other's feelings*
> *Wondering*
> *Mental blocks*
> *Misunderstandings*
> *Having to explain*
> *Striving to understand each other*
> *Different values*
> *Trying to be open-minded trying to listen*
> *And be heard...maybe*
> *Accepted and accepting*
> *Cloudy reasoning —*
> *Struggling with the cloud*
> *With each other.*

Upon completion, the poem was entitled "Our Group" to signify a sense of cohesion and intimacy. Feelings were more openly expressed, and group member interaction was accelerated. Members exhibited mutual concern through the collaborative poem and their investment in the group.

Fifth session

In this session, issues of honesty and individual freedoms emerged. Members continued to discuss the effect of depression on their interpersonal relationships and personal goals. Dan Hill's song "Sometimes When We Touch" (Hill and Mann, 1977) was utilized to deal with some of the pain in communicating on an intimate level. Group members developed mutual support, while each person continued to self-disclose.

The collaborative poem "Loose Ends" reflected a greater sense of cohesion as each member worked toward differentiation.

Loose Ends
Feelings suspended in air
Vulnerable, uncertain.
Every question raises a few more.
Something stuck in my throat
As I dash for a finish line
That I can't see
Closing off the passage ways
Of the maze
And risking new and old directions.
Meeting my other self…
Turning my back on the closed
Passage ways.
While I'm looking over my shoulder
Yes, a sense of regret — a tearful hurt
But,
There's a fulfillment in our own abilities
To answer our own questions.

Indeed, the loose ends could be recognized and accepted. Rather than an obsession with the uncertainties, members could deal with problems in a constructive manner. With the end of group treatment becoming increasingly imminent, group members were becoming more active. They were developing a sense of power and control over their own lives. As a result, depressive behaviors were reduced.

Sixth session

Perceptions of relationships appeared to be the dominant theme of this session. One single female talked about a relationship she was having with a married male. She had ambivalent feelings about continuing the relationship and sought feedback from the group. Although group members were cautious on the matter, they related to the struggle. Members discussed "ideal relationships" and the difficulties of finding a mate. Dan Hill's (1979) song "Perfect Man" was utilized to further develop the group's concerns. The song contains lines pertaining to disillusionment and despair. Issues of perceptions and meeting personal needs were included in the discussion.

The collaborative poem was entitled "Games" and again reflected the theme of the session and indicated the universality of feeling.

Games
We all play games with ourselves
As well as with others…
We are the game.

We decide.
We play the game.
We survive.

The group was working into the final stage of separation and exhibited some regressive behavior with a superficial discussion of relationships and, perhaps, a denial of the group coming to an end the following week, as indicated by: "We decide./...We survive."

Final session

Richard Aldington's (1963) poem "New Love" was used in this final session to help deal with issues of termination and separation. This poem deals with pain as a part of growth. Cashman and West's (1974) song "Lifesong" contains elements of determination and hope and provided a sense of validation and determination for the group. Indeed, group members had found their voice and were able to act on their thoughts and feelings.

Group members had difficulty agreeing on the title of the collaborative poem, but they finally decided:

> **Our Group**
> *No real answers.*
> *Trying not to build a wall*
> *So high that we can't see over*
> *But high enough*
> *To protect our soft spots.*
> *Looking for friends*
> *With whom we can share our soft spots.*
> *Loving*
> *Is being vulnerable.*
> *We alternate*
> *Between building up*
> *And tearing down our walls.*

This poem provided closure for the group. They recognized the continuing struggle between wanting to remain in a safe place and wanting to experience growth. They were in more control and could continue the search if they wished. Termination became a discussion of both finished and unfinished work within a time frame. Both group treatment and poetry are defined within boundaries; however, both remain timeless and unfinished. The client completes the poem or treatment session in his or her own time and space. The group can be just a beginning.

Comment

The use of poetry and pop music was helpful in stimulating group interaction and treating the interpersonal aspects of depression. This is especially helpful in considering the low energy level of depressed clients. Of particular note, the use of poetry and music was helpful in accelerating or decelerating the pace of a session. In essence, the rhythm of a poem or melody of a song could affect time in a therapeutic way. Many of the members were preoccupied with negative thoughts and self-defeating behaviors ("I'm worthless" or "I might as well stay at home"). Through poetry and/or music, the group leaders were able to reach members through cognitive processes that subsequently had impact on affective and behavioral processes. The poem and/or song seemed to tap quickly into the affective realm of individuals, bringing feelings to the surface. For example, when one member verbalized that he wanted to be left alone, a song entitled "So You Couldn't Get to Me" was played. This stimulated group discussion, and subsequently this quiet member began to reveal some painful experiences. Toward the end of the session, he became the recorder for the collaborative poem (he got out of his seat and wrote down the lines), thus increasing his commitment and energy level and helping many other members feel connected. The poetry and music were also helpful in universalizing many of the feelings clients experienced (e.g., "Brooding" and its lines about never being good enough). The use of poetry and music was helpful in bringing some members out of a preoccupation with time past to an active stance in time present.

The timing of having the group members work together to write the collaborative poems toward the end of each session appeared to advance group cohesion at a rather rapid pace. Providing copies of the members' collaborative poems in the subsequent weeks also helped provide continuity between sessions. One especially interesting finding was the similarity between content of the collaborative poems and group developmental stages. Taking into consideration the stages of development observed by Garland et al. (1965), the following comparisons can be made regarding this group's collaborative poems:

- Week 1 — *Pre-affiliation:* "Inside a sinkhole/Dark, grasping/ Don't want to do anything."
- Week 2 — *Power and control:* "Anger/Throwing stones at the moon/Energy not directed well."
- Week 3 — *Intimacy:* "Relief/Is voicing/What you've been afraid to say."
- Week 4 — *Intimacy:* "Delving into each other's feelings/...Struggling with the cloud/Grabbing each other."

- Week 5 — *Differentiation:* "There's a fulfillment in our own abilities/To answer our own questions."
- Week 6 — *Separation:* "Empty interactions/A waste of time/ ...Games are a way of life/A way to survive."
- Week 7 — *Separation/termination:* "Undecided about my feelings/But a little bit better equipped to share."

This may suggest that the collaborative poem, although an imposed structure on the group, enhanced and accelerated group development rather than impeding it. This technique was especially helpful in the time-limited modality (in this case, 7 weeks) by quickly involving members in a concrete shared experience, thus advancing cohesion.

The use of poetry and/or music in group treatment has limitations and requires a careful assessment of group development and individual needs before being utilized. The timing and amount of time spent using poetic techniques is especially important. To be effective, the poetic material must be seen by group members as connected to their processes. This can prompt here-and-now discussion; however, too much time can be spent on a poem or song. Some poems or songs may be aversive to members or may evoke feelings they might not be ready to encounter. In instances when this happens, the variable of time itself can be helpful. Through the leader or through group forces the individual could be supported with the notion that she or he had control over the use of time and was free to choose not to deal with those feelings at that time. This type of decision provides a boundary for feelings and may restore a sense of independence.

Poems or songs can also provide a means to remain withdrawn (i.e., escape). It is perhaps especially important to observe the effect on more silent members (e.g., nonverbal behaviors). This is one area when it is especially helpful to have co-leaders. The use of preexisting poems can inadvertently force rather than facilitate group process if group leaders are insistent upon using a particular poem or song in a given session, perhaps serving the needs of the leader(s) rather than the members. The intention of this poetic technique is to facilitate, not substitute for, group content and process. This perspective avoids a literary or educational emphasis.

Poetry and music appear to have potential as *ancillary* therapeutic group techniques; they are not considered therapeutic entities themselves in this chapter. Poetry and music were especially helpful in working with the clients at the university counseling center by enhancing early engagement in short-term group treatment through a nonthreatening medium. The collaborative poems were instrumental in advancing group cohesion and served as a form of ritual for termination. The collaborative poems were not only useful in connecting sessions, but also, more importantly, in connecting people in a relatively brief period of time. For the group leaders who are comfortable with a facilitative stance that includes use of the arts, poetry and music are additional techniques that may prove valuable in reaching cognitive, affective, and behavioral domains and subsequently advancing group process.

By relating to and taking strength from personally meaningful poetry or music, group members have been able to reduce dependency on the group leaders. Group members have found methods to deal with depression and other problems from within themselves and through each other. The poems or song lyrics provide the necessary boundaries or structure for what can sometimes be confusing and ambivalent feelings. The final collaborative poem written by the group discussed above included a review of boundaries ("Between building up/And tearing down our walls") and the willingness to risk ("Looking for friends/With whom we can share our soft spots").

The group treatment session constitutes only a fragment of a client's week. Through the use of time, poetry, and music, group leaders can help clients maximize their therapeutic experience and can create the means for continued progress beyond the session itself. The structure, measure, and movement of time, poetry, and music have proven to be most compatible with group processes and treatment.

part three

Special topics

chapter five

Working with children

The use of the language arts in therapeutic capacities with children has received significant attention in the professional literature (e.g., Abell, 1998; Brand, 1987; DeMaria, 1991; Gladding, 1987); however, this is not a new concept. *The Junior Poetry Cure: A First-Aid Kit of Verse for the Young of All Ages* by Robert Haven Schauffler (1931) was an early and significant contribution to the literature on poetry as prevention for "unwelcome and painful moods, traits, and habits" (p. xiii). Schauffler put together an anthology of poetry for children organized along several themes in a prescriptive format.

Schauffler used one of the themes, sportsmanship, to encompass five qualities applicable to everyday life: (1) fair play, (2) team work, (3) graceful winning, (4) gallant losing, and (5) persistence. For example, Rudyard Kipling's poem "If" was included in the category of "Sportsmanship Tonics for Fair Play (Poems of Honor)". Other themes addressed the imagination ("Z Rays from Aladdin's Lamp"), energy ("Vitamins"), sadness ("Sunbaths To Fade the Blues — Poems with a Smile"), insight ("Vision Sharpener and Divining Rods — Poems of Deeper Understanding"), and humor ("The Big Medicine of Laughter — Funny Poems"). The organizational framework and many of the poems included in the book, published nearly 70 years ago, still hold value for today. When working with children, multiple modalities should be considered, including individual, family, and group treatment. The model and therapeutic techniques designed for children can be preventive or remedial, all within a developmental context.

Thompson and Rudolph (1992) used two dimensions to examine techniques appropriate for use in counseling children: children's conflicts with others (external) and children's conflicts with self (internal). Some of the poetic approaches to counseling will be briefly reviewed.

Fighting, cruelty, complaining, and resistant behavior are among the external problems for children, and their etiology may be multifaceted (e.g., wanting attention, learned coping mechanisms, poor social skills). One poetic technique is to have each child involved in a fight write his or her side of the story. The story can be recited in person or into a tape recorder and can serve as a basis for discussion, evaluation, and planning (Collins and Collins, 1975; cited in Thompson and Rudolph, 1992). The use of telling a story in private allows the child a safe distance to express feelings and can serve as an emotional release. Later, when it is shared with the clinician, the story provides a springboard for therapeutic work. This technique can, of course, be used by parents and teachers in their respective contexts. The use of a "graffiti sheet" in a child's room can also be supported. This allows the child an opportunity to write out offensive language in a private and controlled setting.

Other poetic techniques suggested by Thompson and Rudolph for external conflicts include the use of stories and films for encouraging discussion about the causes and consequences of fighting. Children can be invited to offer alternative approaches that specific characters could have taken. Poetry and music can be used as relaxation techniques, and traditional bibliotherapy can be used by recommending child-rearing books to parents or books for parents to read to their children that offer a lesson.

Among the internal conflicts (or "conflicts with self") are poor self-concept, underachievement, inattention, shyness, anxiety, dependency, perfectionist behavior, and school phobia. Some of the poetic techniques offered by Thompson and Rudolph (1992) include:

1. Ask the child to write ten positive things about him or herself (e.g., can run fast, is kind toward animals). Consistent with cognitive theory, this technique, if used consistently, could increase positive feelings about self.

2. Use diaries, drawings, sentence stems, and storytelling as a means for understanding the child's thoughts and feelings.

3. For problems such as cheating, a film or story could be used for discussion; subsequently, children can be involved in a role play or puppet-play about cheating.

4. For problems such as truancy, a child could be asked to develop an essay or story to answer the question, "What does it take to make it through life?" This task could lead to a discussion about skills and abilities necessary for the child's imagined adult world.

5. For problems such as inattention due to daydreaming, a child could be asked to write out the daydream. This task could lead into a specific learning exercise.

All of these techniques must, of course, be used with caution and require a careful assessment/diagnosis.

Claudia Gafford Stiles (1995), a special education teacher, wrote a narrative on the use of *The Hill That Grew*, a book by Meeks (1959), and letter writing to help Bobby, a 10-year-old boy, with problems relating to "whining, intrusions, complaints, and demands" (p. 90). Stiles noted that Bobby was upset because time ran out before he took his turn to speak in a group designed to allow children to talk about the books they read that week. A girl in the group spoke about Meeks' story of children who received sleds for Christmas; however, there were no hills in the area where they lived so they could not enjoy their gifts. The children got together and asked the mayor and community for their help. The result was that the town built a hill for them. Bobby was angry that he did not get his opportunity to speak, taking it as a personal affront and displacing his anger on the teacher. *The Hill That Grew* was used to relate to Bobby's plight. Bobby was asked about how the children in the story felt about having sleds but no hill. What did they do? Finally, Bobby was asked what he could do about his situation. Bobby decided to write a letter requesting permission from his regular teacher for extended time in the reading room. The letter writing also involved a process whereby he could rewrite what had been a blaming and angry letter so that it made a reasonable and legitimate request. Bobby later asked to borrow the book and also learned a lesson in "making things happen".

The above is just a brief look at how poetic approaches can be incorporated into practice with children. The following section of this chapter will look at poetry therapy as prevention by examining poetry and career fantasy, and then treatment by looking at poetry therapy and abused children.

*Prevention: career fantasy**

The use of career fantasy with elementary school children can be helpful in promoting health and well-being. When career development is considered as part of human development (Super, 1957), a review of children's career functions and an explanation of their sources could prove helpful in both educational and therapeutic capacities.

Ginzberg et al. (1951) described a particular fantasy period in the career process as occurring in childhood up to the age of approximately 10 years. Ginzberg (1972), in a later reformulation, noted the

---

* This section was developed from an earlier work, Mazza, N. and Mazza, J. (1982) Elementary school children and career fantasy: patterns, procedures, and implications, in *Viewpoints in Teaching and Learning*, Vol. 58, Bloomington, IN: School of Education, Indiana University.

importance of fantasy across age lines. It is important to distinguish career fantasy from career awareness. With career fantasy, one is free to be anything without economic, social, or intellectual restraints. The child may choose what might be fun and is also free to have a change of mind. Career awareness, however, has more to do with what types of jobs are available and exposing the child to different career possibilities. This distinction is not without limitations. Leonard (1971) supports the notion that the child in the fantasy period has the ability to become whatever he or she wishes to become but notes that the child must be exposed to various careers in order to engage in fantasy.

Overview of literature

A review of the literature on children's career fantasy patterns yields very few empirical studies. The literature on early childhood vocational behavior is especially limited, and studies that have dealt with early- and middle-school children had small sample sizes (Vondracek and Kirchner, 1974). In a meta-analysis of 12 studies published between 1983 and 1996, Baker and Taylor (1998) found that the effects of career education interventions for children and adolescents were modest.

Sex-role stereotyping is an often-discussed topic in studies dealing with children and career development. In a study with preschool children, Vondracek and Kirchner (1974) found that, while there is no substantial difference between males and females in the ability to project into the vocational future, the patterns do differ. Male expressions indicated a move toward general adult status, while female expressions were linked more often to the role of parent. Looft (1971a,b) reported similar findings with regard to females aspiring more often than males to the role of parent.

Vondracek and Kirchner (1971a; 1971b) also note that in studies with older females the narrow range in choice of occupations may best be described by Looft as "occupational foreclosure". Vondracek and Kirchner state that foreclosure may already be in operation at the preschool level. One specific indicator of the occupational foreclosure process was noted in terms of females giving fewer career fantasy responses than males. Rosenthal and Chapman (1980, p. 138) caution that "asking children to specify their occupational choice is a relatively crude measure of occupational stereotyping." The authors note that young children have a limited number of occupational choices available and may select only the more salient ones. McMahon and Patton (1997), in examining the career development experiences of children and adolescents in Australia, found that they generally presented stereotypical perceptions.

Studying the occupational interests of rural kindergarten children, Swick and Carlton (1974) noted the importance of the reading process, both verbal and nonverbal, as a means of developing career awareness. Weinger (1998) studied impoverished children's perceptions of career opportunities (12 Caucasian, 12 African-American) and found that they recognized career limitations in being poor and gave indications of feeling hopeless. The importance of developing techniques to increase children's belief in themselves and their future was noted.

Children's literature

One area that warrants investigation is the effect of children's literature on career fantasies. Literature is an extremely powerful vehicle for developing a child's identification with sex-role behavior (Hillman, 1976). It is important to examine whether or not children's literature is consistent with the real world. If one considers literature as a socializing agent, it has a profound effect on children in relation to career aspirations. Distortions and misconceptions in the texts could be part of the foundation for vocational maladjustment.

Knell and Winer (1979) found a great deal of empirical evidence in the literature supporting the idea that selected reading material can influence a child's attitude and behavior. The authors also cite numerous sources confirming strong sex biases in children's literature and raise the question as to why there are so few studies dealing with the effect that reading material has on sex-role stereotyping and attitude formation. Similarly, questions can be raised with respect to ethical and cultural issues.

Career stereotypes can indeed have a negative effect on children by either distorting or limiting opportunities, as well as limiting an appreciation of various careers. Fantasies can be a significant indicator of how children are perceiving and acting upon such stereotypes.

Techniques

One of the primary techniques that can be used in a career fantasy exercise includes asking children to describe in writing or art what he or she would like to be. One variation of this method involves poetry. The use of poetry can be an excellent vehicle to move from the real world to one of fantasy. Children's own poetry can be utilized in a nonthreatening way through the collaborative poem. The poem starts with a general topic such as "If I could be..." and the students are then encouraged to contribute lines. Consider the following example of a collaborative poem:

If I could be a lifeguard...
I would rescue people to shore
And yell "Shark! Here comes one more!"

I could be a mechanic
And fix race cars.
Or be a police officer.
Or even a track star.
I could be a football pro.
Or a farmer
And make things grow.
I could be a nurse
Rushing in and out of doors.
Or a zoo keeper
Listening to the lions roar.
I could be a speed skater.
Or a writer
To write plays.
Or even a lawyer
One of these days.
I could serve in the armed forces.
Or be a daredevil
And do dangerous stunts.
I could be a clogger or Miss USA.
Or a vet to take care of animals all day.
I might be a baseball player
And hit balls far away.
All these things I wish I could be
But right now
I just want to be me.

This poem was created by a fourth-grade class in northern Florida that is largely heterogeneous. The poem listed numerous career possibilities, thus has the potential to expand career awareness via the children's own resources. This may not be the case in all situations. The teacher or counselor may want to read or recommend stories, poems, songs, etc., to begin the process. *The Bookfinder* books (Dreyer, 1977, 1992) and *The Liberty Cap: A Catalogue of Nonsexist Materials for Children* (Davis, 1977) are just two bibliographic resources available as aids in locating such material. The teacher or counselor on occasion may also want to examine the sources of a career fantasy with a particular child (e.g., finding out whether the child knows any mechanics). At this time the exercise is considered primarily as a catalyst.

A development of, or alternative to, the collaborative poem is a technique that calls for children to write individual poems about a career fantasy (to lessen the threat, the teacher or counselor may want to free the child from having to rhyme). Consider the following (unedited) poem by a fourth-grade girl:

When I grow up I think I'll be
A repair person who fixes
Things like these,
Lamps, phones, or even cars.
I could be in movies
And become a movie star.
I could be a track star and
Run all kinds of races.
Or even a beautician
And fix old ladies faces.
But best of all I want
To be myself.

This poem incorporates a number of features or topics found in the other students' poems. The poem is relatively nonsexist (e.g., repair person) and considers a number of possibilities for the individual. Perhaps the most interesting point is the child's concern with "being me". This concern was also present in the collaborative poem above.

Assessment of children's self-concepts and the promotion of healthy ones can indeed be unique endeavors. Poems are expressions of self drawn from one's own inner resources, and career fantasies offer the opportunity for development of this self. Art and poetry both can be used as vehicles for healthy expression and exploration of children's career fantasies. It is not the specific fantasy that necessarily has to be nurtured, but rather the child's ability and enthusiasm to engage in such fantasies.

While there are many excellent new career/vocational kits and training packages available, teachers and counselors very often face budgetary and time restraints that make it difficult to either obtain or utilize these resources. The techniques described are surely not new but are economical, practical, and easily incorporated. The techniques can be linked to a variety of educational and counseling objectives. For the counselor, a consideration of career fantasy may yield information about self-concept as well as family or social dynamics influencing a child's performance. The techniques are necessarily portable and can be used differentially.

Treatment: child abuse*

It is often difficult to adapt conventional therapies to the treatment of abused children and their families. Naitove (1982) noted that sexually

---

* This section was developed from an earlier work, Mazza, N., Magaz, C., and Scaturro, J. (1987) Poetry therapy with abused children, in *The Arts in Psychotherapy*, 14, 85–92.

abused children frequently perceive the usual verbal methods of assessment and treatment as threatening. Children may not have the cognitive or emotional development requisite for effective use of the interventions. A consideration of the child's basic personality, age, sex, developmental level, family, and environment, as well as the history and specifics of the traumatic event is necessary in order to understand the child's current functioning (Kempe and Kempe, 1984; Sgroi, 1982). Children who are victims of abuse will have difficulties forming relationships, including the therapeutic one. They may have expectations of violence and rejection (Green, 1978). The aforementioned points suggest that maintaining the creative use of resources for individualized assessment and treatment is important in a time of increased demand for services and limited personnel (Hovda, 1977). The use of the poetic is one resource that will be explored in terms of technique and as an approach to practice.

The treatment of abused children requires an interagency and multidisciplinary approach that involves the family and social system. This section, however, will be limited to an examination of the use of poetry therapy in the individual and group treatment of abused children. The utilization of the poetic in clinical practice must be consistent with program objectives (e.g., build trust, provide sense of safety, improve communication and socialization skills, raise self-esteem) and a therapeutic orientation. Poetry therapy will be considered in both expressive (writing, speaking) and receptive (reading, listening) modes.

Clinical considerations

The use of poetry in the treatment of abused children requires caution. In her discussion of the use of printmaking, Stember (1977) noted that abused children have fears about being hit for not doing things correctly. The abused child often suppresses curiosity and independent action out of fear of punishment. Harry Chapin (1978) perhaps best illustrates this point in "Flowers Are Red", a song about a young boy who starts school with excitement about drawing but is subsequently reprimanded by his teacher because it was not time for art and he had chosen the wrong colors for the flowers and leaves. The boy's protest is met with the punishment of being put in a corner until he could get it "right". The frightened child finally succumbs. This performance issue can curtail any new undertaking; therefore, in introducing poetry it is essential to emphasize feelings, images, and sounds rather than literary mechanics.

Children are natural poets who will create if the necessary preconditions of permission and encouragement are present. Poetry writing is a unique way of expressing one's self. The child's reaction to a preexisting poem is also a unique poetic expression. All poems can be considered incomplete, and the child completes the poem with his or her unique response. For the abused child who is feeling fragmented, the sense of wholeness reflected in his or her response to the poetry has a healing quality.

Preexisting poems

When utilizing preexisting poems, the therapist must anticipate and be willing to explore the child's reactions. This process can begin by the therapist examining her or his own reactions to the poem. The concern is that the child will reach unspoken conclusions that are counterproductive (e.g., guilt). Any given poem might also bring up feelings the child is not prepared to deal with at the time. Inviting discussion and the possibility of different endings or changes in the preexisting poem can also aid in the assessment process and further problem-solving activity. The poem essentially becomes a springboard for the expression of feelings. Children may be invited to respond to the entire poem, or a specific line or image.

Selection of poetic material must be consistent with the therapeutic purpose. For example, Silverstein's (1974) "Treehouse" could be utilized with an abused child in the early stages of treatment to facilitate self-expression. The poem includes the lines "A treehouse, a free house/ A secret you and me house" (p. 79). Houses, trees, and people are among the subjects chosen most frequently by children who have been asked to draw spontaneously (Wohl and Kaufman, 1985). This poem, therefore, could be used in conjunction with an art exercise or as a point of departure for a discussion of home and family. "Masks" by Giovanni (1980) is another poem that is suitable for both art and discussion exercises. Facilitative questions would include, "Would you draw a picture of that mask?" and "What kind of mask do you like to wear?"

Poetry writing (including oral creations)

For abused children, poetry offers a channel for speaking of feelings when all other channels appear closed. Sources for prestructuring some of the poetry writing include Joseph's (1969) organizational framework of *The Me Nobody Knows* (i.e., how the children see themselves, how they see their neighborhoods and the world outside, and things they cannot touch) and Koch's (1970, 1973) numerous techniques to teach poetry writing to children (e.g., writing a poem in which every line begins with "I wish..."). Group creative writing is an additional therapeutic technique that can promote self-awareness and group interaction as well as increase self-esteem (Buck and Kramer, 1974; Lauer and Goldfield, 1970; Mazza, 1981b).

Case example

Group

Time-limited groups can be particularly helpful to children who have been victims of sexual abuse (Rose, 1985). Overall, the length of treatment will depend on several factors, including severity of the trauma and degree of emotional support available by significant others (Porter et al., 1982). However, even in long-term therapy, the brief treatment group can be one part of a comprehensive treatment plan. The preferred form of therapy for sexually abused school-age children is groups offering elements of universalization, diagnostic information regarding children's social skills and fantasies, and opportunities for problem solving (Kempe and Kempe, 1984).

The following example is from a time-limited group (50-minute weekly sessions for 6 weeks) for first- and second-grade sexually abused children (four girls, two boys). It was largely homogeneous with respect to lower socioeconomic status and was conducted in a school setting by a social worker from the Child Protection Team. The purpose of the group was to provide support, improve socialization skills, and raise the self-esteem of the members.

A feeling word exercise was introduced early in the third session of the group. The following words were listed (with brightly colored markers) across the top of a flip-chart: *sad, glad, mad*. Children were asked to list other words that could be used to describe these emotions. Later, the children were put in dyads and given assorted magazines. They were asked to cut out pictures that express feeling words and paste them on a poster board. Upon completion of the task, members of each dyad shared their poster with the entire group. The collaborative poem was introduced later to conclude the session. All members of the group were invited to contribute to the poem. The group leader wrote the words on the flip-chart as they were contributed. The following poem was created:

> *What makes you happy?*
> *When I enjoy myself.*
> *I like to smile and it's*
> *Joyful to smile*
> *And I like to love all the while.*
> *I cry when I'm sad.*
> *Why do you?*
> *My brother is bad*
> *When he makes me black and blue.*
> *Mad is sad and you are bad.*
> *Once I was mad at my dad*

Chapter five: Working with children   *71*

And my dad was sad 'cause he
Loves me.
Once I was afraid
My roommate disappeared.
A scary show I made.
But when my mom came
I had no fear.

The secret club

Several salient points regarding the construction of the poem should be noted:

1. Each person in the group contributed a minimum of one line.
2. Both verbal behaviors (using connecting words such as "and" and asking for feelings) and nonverbal behaviors (writing on the chart with brightly colored markers, eye contact, facial expressions) contributed to the development of the poem (including participation by two members who had been silent in previous sessions).
3. The group signed their poem "The Secret Club".
4. Although advised the poem did not have to rhyme, the children chose the traditional structure. Perhaps this was a function of safety, familiarity, or just playfulness.

It appears that the poem was helpful in universalizing feelings. It was a nonthreatening device that enabled group members to share feelings. By ostensibly talking about the poem, they were talking about themselves. The children recognized they were not alone in experiencing some of the following impact issues (Porter et al., 1982):

*   Depression: "I cry when I'm sad."
*   Anger and guilt: "Once I was mad at my dad/And my dad was sad..."
*   Fear: "Once I was afraid/My roommate disappeared."

The element of hope is in the ability of group members to externalize their feelings. By putting feelings into written words, group members gained a sense of mastery and control. The choice of signing the poem "The Secret Club" also provided a sense of identity and was a reaffirmation of the group. Additionally, issues of confidentiality and trust became solidified. Perhaps one of the most significant effects was the fostering of group cohesion, the feeling of "we" in creating a product. Essentially the poem contributed to the group process and was consistent with a middle stage of group development.

Comment

Drawing from Lerner (1982), the emphasis in this chapter has been on the poetry *in* therapy. The challenge and direction of all creative arts therapies were issued by Johnson (1986, p. 3): "No longer do we write exclusively about the therapy session, rather we write directly about issues such as divorce, child abuse, psychosis, or alcoholism." With this perspective, the recommendations for research in the area of poetry therapy and child abuse include:

1. Use of poetry as a medium when providing consultation, training, and education in the dynamics of child abuse to helping professionals.
2. Development of poetic resources that can be utilized in the prevention and treatment of all forms of child abuse. This includes ethnic- and gender-sensitive material. There is also the issue of accessibility. Perhaps in the tradition of Meals on Wheels and Stember's (1977) artmobile, Poetry on Wheels could be added.
3. Systematic qualitative and quantitative evaluation of poetic approaches with abused children and their families.
4. Further investigation of the complementary use of poetry with other art forms (e.g., art, music, dance) in the assessment and treatment process.
5. Examination of literary influences on child abuse (including research on children's reading experiences).
6. Examination of literary influences (including lyrics of pop music) used as coping mechanisms.
7. Precise reports dealing with the use of poetry for specific types of abuse (e.g., incest).

The differential use of poetry in the treatment of abused children has promise as an ego-supportive technique that facilitates self-expression and fosters a sense of validation and control. In group modalities, the promise of poetry relates specifically to cohesion, universalization, and self-expression.

Planning an effective treatment program that includes poetry is contingent upon detailed assessment. This is one area where poetry can enhance and/or build upon an initial assessment through art therapy. Art is particularly useful in the early stages of therapy when the verbal accessibility of the young child is limited by both developmental level and the traumatic event (Wohl and Kaufman, 1985). Poetry can be especially helpful in the middle and later stages of therapy when some trust has been established and the child is more likely to verbalize. On the other hand, poetry and popular music can be helpful in breaking resistance in the early stages of treatment (Mazza, 1979, 1981a). At this point in time, the data are insufficient to formulate any direct guidelines with respect to the stages of treatment except to suggest the importance of flexibility. Leedy and Rapp (1973) noted the connection between art and poetry therapy in that both forms have the potential to release feelings via creation.

Poetry and art are both useful in capitalizing on childhood fantasies (Mazza and Mazza, 1982), and the combined use of poetry and music in therapy can motivate and activate clients (Mazza and Prescott, 1981; Mazza and Price, 1985). Naitove (1982) noted that poetic and musical activities might be especially suitable for some auditory attenders, while visual attenders would be more responsive to graphic and plastic arts. The overall use of poetry and other art forms offers a therapeutic element of play to the child that serves the therapist in both diagnostic and treatment capacities.

The potential of the poetic in helping the therapist establish a nurturing and constant relationship with the abused child comes from two levels that recognize the poetic process as well as specific techniques. Papp (1984, p.260) wrote, "The primary material a therapist has to work with is the poetry in people, and we would do well to let it guide us in our work with them." The poetry within children speaks to the pain and promise of the therapeutic growth process.

chapter six

Poetry therapy and
adolescent suicide*

The therapeutic capacity of the language arts for adolescents has also received significant attention in the literature (e.g., Abell, 1998; Bowman, 1992; Cohen-Morales, 1989; DeMaria, 1991; Holman, 1996; Mazza, 1981b; Mazza, 1991a; Roscoe et al., 1985). The purpose of this chapter is to explore the role of poetry in the prevention of suicide, with particular attention paid to the aspects of choice and decision making as they relate to both poetry and therapy. The ego-enhancing qualities of decision making can improve self-esteem, contribute to healthy identity formation, and restore an element of control to the adolescent during a tumultuous transitional period. It is also clear that the perception of having no adequate alternatives to solve specific problems is a contributing factor in adolescent suicide attempts.

The underlying assumption in this chapter is that, through poetry writing and other forms of written communication, adolescents can project aspects of themselves. Earlier studies have indicated that poetry is useful as a means for adolescents to explore and cope with their feelings. Jon Shaw (1981) noted that the adolescent period is one of high creativity; however, as the adolescent gains increasing independence, this period is accompanied by a sense of object loss. He further suggested that themes of time, loss, and death in the adolescent poetry of such famous poets as Alfred Edward Houseman, Edgar Allan Poe, and Sylvia Plath indicate an interrelationship among creativity, mourning, and adolescence.

Adolescents often express their private thoughts and feelings in their writings. In *Vivienne: The Life and Suicide of an Adolescent Girl*, John Mack and Holly Hickler (1981) examined a 14-year-old girl's diary ("My Private Paper Book"), poems, school compositions, and letters in

---

* An earlier version of this chapter was published in Deats, S.M. and Lenker, L.T., Eds. (1989) *Youth Suicide Prevention: Lessons from Literature*, New York: Plenum Press.

an effort to understand what led this bright and seemingly successful young person to hang herself. In explaining her disclosure of Vivienne's suicide, the girl's mother stated, "I wanted other young people to know she shared their pain. But I wanted them to find a different answer" (p. 122). One of the possible answers is the securing of some form of psychotherapy that includes poetic elements.

Use of preexisting poems and song lyrics

As noted previously, one of the more common techniques employed within the receptive/prescriptive mode of poetry therapy is the use of preexisting poems. The selection of a poem may be based on the isoprinciple of choosing a poem with a mood similar to that of the client but one that offers a positive message (Leedy, 1969c). Another method of selection is the use of an open-ended poem in which a number of diverse reactions could be anticipated. The poem then serves as an interpersonal vehicle for clients (Lerner, 1975). Leedy cautions therapists that with depressed and potentially suicidal clients poems that offer no hope, increase guilt, or advocate the seeking of vengeance should not be used. The hopeful message could, indeed, be developed through an emotional identification with the poem; however, if the positive message is contrived or didactic, it may serve only to invalidate the client's feelings.

The very form and structure of a poem can provide a sense of control which may make the reader feel less alone even if there is not a hopeful message in the poem. It is imperative for the therapist to anticipate a number of reactions. Indeed, one alternative perceived by the adolescent could be suicide. Such an alternative, however, should be discussed in light of its being a permanent solution to a temporary problem. In response to one poem, an adolescent reported that he had decided to go away to college rather than stay at home with his chronically ill father. However, this decision also involved leaving behind his girlfriend. He viewed both roads (staying or going) as being one way, fearing that once a road was taken he could not return. The issue of leaving behind people and places was subsequently addressed, and the future as well as the past were explored through discussing such things as new places he would see, experiences he has had, and his friends. Although the future was uncertain, the client's creativity was identified as a source of strength to help him pass successfully through difficult times.

Isoprinciple without positive message

"The World Is Not a Pleasant Place To Be" by Nikki Giovanni (1972) could be useful in the suicide assessment phase of working with an adolescent by encouraging the client to talk about feelings of loneliness, loss, and despair. Sharing this poem could also provide the means for the client to at least talk about suicide, a vital precondition to preventing it. By talking about the pain expressed in the poem, the adolescent begins to share personal feelings. Specific suicide assessment questions could be used by the therapist. For example, when using "The World Is Not a Pleasant Place To Be" the therapist could ask, "Have you been in so much pain in your world that you have thought of killing yourself?" If the client answers "yes", then the therapist could ask, "How would you do it?" Building upon a line in the poem relating to the need to be held by someone, the question of who would be the most affected by the adolescent's death could be addressed. Extreme caution should be exercised when Giovanni's poem is introduced, because the adolescent might conclude that suicide is a viable alternative.

The close connection between poetry and popular music might also be taken advantage of. Introducing Janis Ian's (1974) "At Seventeen" could help to establish a close connection with the adolescent client. The feelings of loneliness and the negative view of self, so common in adolescence, could be discussed with reference to Ian's song, which has the potential to universalize feelings.

Isoprinciple with positive message

The issue of self-worth could be addressed in a positive and unique manner through the use of Virginia Satir's (1975) poem "I Am Me", which includes lines relating to self-respect, self-esteem, problem solving, resourcefulness, and intimacy:*

> But as long as
> I am friendly
> And loving to myself,
> I can
> ...look for the
> Solution to
> The puzzles and
> For ways to find
> Out more about me...
> I have the tools
> To survive
> To be
> Close to others
> To be productive.

---

* Excerpt from Satir, V. (1975) *Self-Esteem*, Berkeley, CA: Celestial Arts. With permission.

Satir wrote this poem for a 15-year-old girl who, while suffering great pain, asked her about the meaning of life. Similarly, Whitney Houston's performance of the song "The Greatest Love of All" (Creed and Masser, 1977) could also be utilized as a source of inspiration. Currently, one of the most powerful songs dealing with depression and suicide is Peter Gabriel and Kate Bush's performance of "Don't Give Up" (Gabriel, 1986). Also, Billy Joel's (1985) "You're Only Human" is perhaps the most direct song treating adolescent suicide in an upbeat manner and offers much hope. On a lighter note, Emily Dickinson's (1861/1959) "I'm Nobody" allows the adolescent to identify with the poet's perspective on success and superficiality.

Creative writing

Within the expressive/creative mode of poetry therapy, the use of poetry writing is especially promising. Bruce Roscoe and his colleagues (1985), in a study of 149 high school students, found that 86% of the participants used at least one form of writing for the purpose of self-expression. Poetry was rated as the most popular form (37.5%), with diaries rated second (33%).

Encouraging adolescents to write and offering to discuss their writings can be useful for both assessment and treatment purposes. The writing could be free writing (any topic, any form) or prestructured (using sentence stems such as "If you knew me..." to develop a poem or prose piece). As noted earlier, Mack and Hickler (1981) studied the written communications of Vivienne, a 14-year-old girl who had committed suicide. According to the two authors of the study, an excerpt from one of her poems expresses Vivienne's sense of futility and hopelessness, relating particularly to the departure of her sixth-grade teacher with whom she had developed a strong attachment. The poem contained an image of "being fenced in" and a feeling that she could not "escape". For the purposes of illustrating technique, Vivienne's poem will be considered from a clinical perspective. If Vivienne had been in therapy and if she had shared the above poem with the therapist, it would have been helpful for the therapist to ask her to talk more about the "fence", as it is easier to talk about a fence or a poem than to talk about oneself. Some facilitative questions in this situation might have included:

1.   How was the fence built?
2.   What might be outside the fence?
3.   What or who is inside the fence?
4.   Is there a gate?

A journal entry of Vivienne's revealed her first attempt to strangle herself. On the back of that entry, Mack and Hickler found a poem about the darkness of a dream ending. Vivienne evoked the pain of feeling that she would not be missed. The dream was drawn and closed.

To match the theme and mood of Vivienne's poem, the therapist might choose to select an earlier published poem, such as Langston Hughes' (1951/1970) "Harlem", which speaks to dreams and destruction. This poem in conjunction with a client's poem could serve to universalize the feelings and tap the reservoir of internal turmoil and despair. The poetry could also provide an outlet for a client's rage.

Vivienne's poetry continued to reveal increasing suicidal danger. One month prior to her suicide, she wrote "And Where Is the Moon?" The poem includes lines portraying a sense of emptiness and desperation. Mack, the clinician who interviewed the family after Vivienne's death and reviewed her writings, concluded that Vivienne suffered several important losses in the year before her death (the departure of a teacher with whom she had developed a strong attachment, a move to a new home, and a change to a different school), that she was extremely sensitive to her family's emotional pain, and that she maintained a very low self-esteem. In short, Vivienne saw no way out of her depression.

In her classic study of adolescent girls in a delinquency institution, Gisela Konopka (1966) invited the inmates to share their writings (e.g., diaries, poems). One 16-year-old girl wrote a poem depicting her life as being filled with pain. She wrote that she would "die alone". Konopka noted that the girl read her poem in a monotone voice to guard against the impact of feeling. A few months prior to the reading, the girl had made a suicide attempt. In a later article, Konopka (1983) uses the poem of an 18-year-old to illustrate the adolescent issues of alienation, anger, poor self-regard, and neglect.

All the feelings that are expressed in each of these two poems are indicative of the potential for a suicide attempt. Konopka notes, however, that diaries and poetry may serve to provide a way out of what seems like hopeless pain. Reluctant to share their feelings with adults, adolescents find peer friendships and writings to be safer vehicles for emotional discharge.

These examples indicate that poetry writing can serve as a vehicle to express painful feelings that could result in suicide for the adolescent. In some cases, poetry saves lives, but in others it serves the limited role of an obituary, recording the psychological erosion of the adolescent leading to suicide.

In *The Therapy of Poetry*, Molly Harrower (1972), a poet and psychologist, reviewed her own poetry and creative endeavors from age 3 to maturity. Harrower's analysis of her adolescent poems helps us to understand in part why one adolescent chooses to live whereas another chooses death as the only viable alternative (p. 27):

> "The poem restores an inner balance by both ac-
> knowledging and going beyond the new infor-
> mation that has to be absorbed. It is as if the poet
> is now entitled to confront life again with opti-
> mism. The disquieting truth has been dealt with."

In the earlier example dealing with Vivienne's writings, Mack and Hickler (1981) noted that the girl absorbed and could not adequately go beyond the pain of family, social, and personal conflicts.

Family and group techniques utilizing creative writing can also be helpful in working with the potentially suicidal adolescent. Miller (1982) noted that suicide is often dyadic in nature; that is, it often involves two people — the suicidal person and the significant other. The use of dyadic poems, in which the task is for two people to develop a two-line poem, can be especially helpful once it is determined which individual would be most affected by the client's suicide. With the therapist playing the role of the significant other, the poem could be developed. In family treatment, the technique could be used with specific subsystems (e.g., father and son).

Family or group collaborative poems could also be developed. This technique involves each member being given the opportunity to contribute one or more lines to a poem. Considering the tremendous influence of peers in the adolescent stage, such group modalities are often very effective. The excerpt that follows is from "Frustration", an adolescent group poem (Mazza, 1981a, p.403):

> *Try like hell to forget about it*
> *And sometimes feel more frustrated.*
> *Can't sleep*
> *Keep thinking*
> *And it keeps coming back.*

The collaborative poem is helpful in getting members to externalize their difficulties. It also engages members in the problem-solving process of creating a poem compatible with the entire group.

Applying reading and writing of poetry to therapy

In my own work with troubled adolescents and their families, I have used poetry as an approach to promoting therapeutic change. In earlier reports, I have documented how poetry and popular music are especially effective with adolescents (Mazza, 1979, 1981; Mazza et al., 1987). The cases that were documented concern alcohol abuse, sexual abuse, and depression. In each case, the introduction of poetry or the lyrics of popular music helped to engage an often initially resistant client. Although the problems presented were very rarely specified as being "suicidal", each of the adolescents gave some indication of a potential risk of self-destruction. Once poetry was validated by the therapist as acceptable, adolescents would often share their poetic preferences and writings. This, of course, is dependent on the level of trust that is established by the therapist.

Case vignettes

Robin, a 17-year-old girl, was being treated for alcohol abuse and depression. Billy Joel's (1973) "Piano Man" was used to relate to the client's feelings of despair and her need to maintain a "front". Emily Dickinson's (1861/1959) "I'm Nobody" was helpful to the client in dealing with identity issues. Although poetry was utilized within the sessions, journal writing also served a therapeutic purpose between sessions. Robin was able to record such feelings as, "Sometimes I think my parents expect too much of me. … My father wanting me to go out with football players when I can't even get anyone to go out with." In part, the client voiced a typical adolescent complaint concerning parental pressures. The written communication that she shared with me in the session allowed her to talk about her view of self and her perceived family pressures. Subsequently, some actions could be taken to instigate change (Mazza, 1979).

Michelle, an 18-year-old being treated for depression, revealed that she read and wrote poetry in addition to keeping a diary. She shared parts of her diary with me, and it revealed not only feelings of her emerging sexuality, parental conflicts, and concern with death, but also feelings of despair. Her poetry revealed a poor self-image, social inadequacies, and intense feelings of insecurity. Michelle also revealed that she had read much of Sylvia Plath's poetry. She reported ambivalent feelings toward a boyfriend whom she had been dating for 2 years. The boyfriend had been inflicting verbal and physical abuse on Michelle. Given the above factors, it appeared that Michelle felt trapped with no alternatives for improving her life. A suicide assessment yielded some ideation; however, at the time, she was a moderate risk. The use of Robert Frost's (1915/1964) "The Road Not Taken" proved fruitful in facilitating Michelle's exploration of alternatives. By providing Michelle with an element of choice, I was able to formulate a treatment contract with her that included her agreement not to commit suicide without first calling me. It also included involving her family in the treatment process (Mazza, 1981a).

Comment

The use of poetry in treatment to prevent adolescent suicide has promise; however, extreme caution is required. The techniques that were described are intended only for skilled therapists (social workers, psychologists, and psychiatrists). Any tool that has the power to help also has the power to harm. Because the poetry of adolescents is a very private matter, clients should not be pressured to share their writing. They may also feel, as many literary scholars do, that poetry should not be analyzed in any psychological manner; it is art rather than therapy, and to violate that sacred trust is abhorrent. The use of published poems might also evoke feelings that the adolescent might not be ready to encounter. Also, there is always danger that the adolescent could construe a self-destructive meaning from a poem. Another danger involved in the use of preselected poems or songs is the client's possible identification with a negative role model, such as, for example, the poet Sylvia Plath, who committed suicide. The danger of a client's romanticizing suicide remains a potential problem.

Suicide is an extreme form of communication (Miller, 1982), and in this chapter I have emphasized expression and communication as the important aspects of poetry that have therapeutic value. Indeed, feelings and language are considered the two basic components of both poetry and therapy (Crootof, 1969). The poetry writing of adolescents can be an invaluable tool in identifying warning signals of suicide, while also serving as an emotional safety valve for the troubled adolescent. The introduction of published poems or popular song lyrics can help establish the crucial connection between client and therapist by providing a relevant and nonthreatening device whereby the adolescent can begin to talk about self-disclosures. The subjective response of a client to a preexisting poem is, of course, shaped by that individual's history and experience; personal meanings are at the core of poetry therapy. However, poetry also has the capacity to universalize feelings. The structure that the poem provides for those feelings can also lend a degree of hope and support to the client. In essence, free-floating anxiety can become anchored, even if for a brief time.

A careful and comprehensive study of adolescent creative writing, particularly diaries and poetry, could yield invaluable data concerning the direct causes of suicide. Perhaps more significantly, research in this area could enlighten us as to what factors prevent the adolescent from committing suicide. If there were more poetry in our lives, perhaps there would be less need for poetry therapy or for any other form of therapy, for that matter. Of necessity, this chapter has been limited to a review of the use of poetic content in relation to the treatment of adolescent suicide and the role of poetry therapy as an ancillary technique in the assessment and treatment process. There are, of course, implications for educators who must identify potentially suicidal adolescents and make appropriate referrals. Similarly, there are implications for parents and concerned others, who must respect and learn from the writing and the poetic/musical interests of adolescents. The challenge now for us all is to keep the adolescent and the poetry alive.

chapter seven

Poetry therapy and battered women*

A Family Matter
She left in the middle of the night
Battered and broken
Leaving it all behind her
With her broken dreams.
"He's really sorry, you know."
Long sleeves and turtlenecks
A little too much make-up
Layers of resignation
Covering purple and scarlet reminders.
"He really couldn't help it."
Secrets to share with no one.
Carefully concealed
Visible to no one's eye
Like the bruise on her heart.
"He promised no more."
A new day will dawn
And she will return
To his empire,
Like a queen to her king
To play the scene over
Again and again.
"But I still love him."
—Judith M. Curran (1989, p. 279)

Judith Curran's poem vividly portrays the cycle of violence in abusive relationships that is so well documented in the professional literature.

---

* An earlier version of this chapter was published in Deats, S.M. and Lenker, L.T., Eds. (1991) *The Aching Hearth: Family Violence in Life and Literature,* New York: Plenum Press.

Barbara Mathias (1986, p. 20) describes family violence as "the slap that is felt for generations." There are many such visions associated with such terms as "spouse abuse", "battered woman", "family/domestic violence", "victim", and "maltreatment", and a few are as poetic as Curran's verse or Mathias's verbal image. Recognizing spouse abuse (including abuse between couples not legally married) as a serious form of family violence, this chapter will explore the surprisingly pertinent role of poetry in understanding and healing battered women.

Torre (1990) discussed drama as a consciousness-raising strategy for the self-empowerment of working women. She noted that drama "is a different way of approaching the truth" (p. 51). Indeed, spouse abuse may be approached very differently by the various professionals or agencies providing service to the victim (e.g., therapist, police officer, physician, shelter worker). Poetry, like drama and other arts, provides another perspective or way of approaching the truth. When the poet is also the victim, the perspective becomes even more compelling.

Battered women's experiences, reactions, and methods of coping with abuse can be expressed through the language and imagery of poetry. Kissman (1989, p. 225) noted that there are numerous examples of women's poetry that show how creativity can be used as a survival mechanism:

> "Women who are isolated with their 'secrets' of battering, rape, and incest can tie into the collective and communal network of the written word which is rich in metaphors about women's experiences."

The publication of poetry in women's shelter or program newsletters across the country is one example of how the network is being strengthened.

Poetry therapy and related arts therapies can be useful adjunctive techniques in the treatment of victims of family violence (Mazza et al., 1987). Crisis intervention is the most common form of treatment for the battered woman and necessarily involves such practical matters as ensuring the safety and well-being of the victim and her children. It should also be noted that the word "crisis" is a very subjective term and that many women at risk would not describe their situation as a crisis. For these women and their families, violence is the norm.

Brief treatment that involves "the planned use of a number of therapeutic interventions aimed at the achievement of limited goals within a limited time frame" (Mazza, 1987a, p. 81) is another appropriate form of treatment for battered women. Given that the helping professional may be working with the victim for only a brief time, poetry therapy can serve as a catalyst to promote change; however, it should be noted that the use of the poetic in clinical practice with battered women must be consistent with both program objectives (e.g., building trust, providing a sense of security, improving self-esteem, developing self-empowerment) and therapeutic orientation.

For the clinician, treatment should include social responsibility for identifying human rights issues and battered women. Those sensitive to their experiences offer a form of qualitative research that compels us to undertake intervention and preventive action. Literary works dealing with spouse abuse challenge us to look at this "private" problem as a public issue. In short, clinical practice and social responsibility are intricately related. The following poetic techniques are useful in working with victims and the larger system of which they are a part.

Preexisting poems

As noted previously, this technique involves reading a carefully selected poem to an individual or group and inviting reactions. Shame and stigma are often associated with being a battered woman; battered women thus frequently feel isolated and alone. Sharing either a poem or a prerecorded piece of music with accompanying lyrics that corresponds to the victim's mood or problem can help validate and universalize the victim's feelings. The poetry can thus serve as a catalyst for self-disclosure and/or group discussion. Tracy Chapman's (1983) song "Behind the Wall" includes lines that deplore the futility of calling the police. This song is a valuable means of allowing victims the opportunity to share their own experiences. By beginning to talk about the song, they inevitably talk about themselves. By emotionally identifying with the song, battered women are able to validate their own experience (e.g., feeling trapped), seek alternative solutions (e.g., in a crisis situation, they might not have time to rely on the police), or dispel myths (e.g., some police departments actually have a pro-arrest policy and are sensitive to victim problems).

"The Road Not Taken" by Robert Frost (1915/1964) is an excellent poem to use in dealing with the pressures of choice a battered woman experiences in trying to decide whether to act or to refrain from taking any new action (separate from her husband, go to a shelter, seek therapy, call the police). The poem can be employed to review with the victim the choices she has made in the past regarding personal, family, and social matters. If she has left her husband in the past, what prompted the decision? What was the outcome? Looking at her current situation, what are her alternatives? If she chooses to stay, what is her safety plan?

Many abused women are able to make an emotional identification with the poem "After a While" (Shoffstall, 1971); the following lines are particularly noteworthy:

> *After a while you learn*
> *The subtle difference*
> *Between*
> *Holding a hand*
> *And chaining a soul.*
> *So you plant your own garden*
> *And decorate*
> *Your own soul*
> *Instead of waiting*
> *For someone to bring you*
> *Flowers.*
> *And you learn*
> *That you really can endure*
> *That you really are strong*
> *And you really have worth.*

The above poem instills hope by identifying common feelings that abused women experience. The poem also calls victims to action and affirms their self-worth.

Creative writing

The use of written self-expression has relevance for both assessment and treatment. Journal or diary entries and poetry provide the victim with a vehicle to express emotion and gain a sense of order and control. Creative writing could also be prestructured through the use of sentence stems such as "When I am alone…" or "If you knew me…". One technique is to create collaborative poems; each group member is given the opportunity to contribute one or more lines to the poem. Following is an excerpt of a collaborative poem written by a women's group that included several survivors of spouse abuse (Mazza, 1988, p. 490):

> *My control*
> *Is my protector*
> *Of my feelings.*
> *It is also my cage*
> *Looking for a balance.*
> *Where?*
> *Inside…*

The collaborative poem generates a feeling of accomplishment and fosters group cohesion. It validates the group's feelings. Copies of the collaborative poem may be made for discussion in a subsequent session. Group members may choose to discuss the poem further, or, at the very least, they have validation of the previous week's work.

The use of journal writing is an especially powerful tool in working with battered women. Fox (1982) and Brand (1979) noted a number of advantages to employing personal documents in therapy, such as the log, diary, or journal. This technique encourages internal examination, increases attention upon self-reporting and observation, provides continuity between therapy sessions, promotes competence through the discipline required to write about oneself, facilitates expression of feelings, and offers a creative outlet. The journal and other writing assignments require that work take place outside the therapy session; however, the review of such material at the discretion of the client allows her control and the opportunity for continuity between sessions.

Metaphors, imagery, and language

Using poetic expression, imagery, or symbols derived from the client's language and experience can also serve a therapeutic function. The May/June 1986 issue of *The Family Therapy Networker* was subtitled "Lifting the Shade on Family Violence" and illustrated accordingly (Mathias, 1986). This image vividly captures the sense of secrecy and isolation obscuring spouse abuse and compels us to expand our vision. In a clinical situation, a person who frequently refers to "home" could be asked to draw, write, or talk about a house. What does it look like? Who is in it? In working with victims of abuse, very powerful images often emerge (e.g., beatings, shattered glass, verbal abuse, arrival of a police car, terrified children). Healing involves the discharge of powerful emotions in a safe environment, with appropriate support and guidance.

Clinical issues

Walker's (1979, 1984, 1987) research identified a three-phase cycle of violence that the battered woman experiences:

1. *The tension-building phase.* In this phase, the woman has some control over the incidence of violence and can perhaps prevent violence by meeting the batterer's domestic demands (such as, keeping the children quiet or making the proper meal). The demands, however, increase and it becomes more difficult to keep the batterer calm. The poem "Just Like Dad" (Curran, 1989, p. 278) makes reference to this stage: "She should know better than to burn the roast./Or say something stupid./Or leave the house without him. ..."
2. *The acute battering incident.* It often occurs without warning. Tracy Chapman's (1983) song "Behind the Wall" includes a reference to screaming in the night that is followed by silence and the arrival of an ambulance.

3. *The kind/loving contrition.* This is often referred to as the "honeymoon" or "hearts and flowers" stage. Tension is reduced following the explosion. The man asks for forgiveness and promises never to hit the woman again. In "A Family Matter" (Curran, 1989, p. 279), the following lines close the first three stanzas: "He's really sorry, you know/.../He really couldn't help it/.../ He promised no more." The last stanza affirms the cycle:

> *A new day will dawn*
> *And she will return*
> *To his empire,*
> *Like a queen to her king*
> *To play the scene over*
> *Again and again.*
> *"But I still love him."*

Walker (1987) noted that there are five basic areas that must be recognized by the helping professional working with battered women: manipulation, expression of anger, dissociation, denial, and compliance. The following will be an examination of each area from a poetic perspective.

Manipulation

Battered women often maintain unrealistic expectations regarding their ability to calm the batterer by doing everything perfectly. Failure to succeed evokes guilt. Alice Walker's (1984) "How Poems Are Made/A Discredited View" addresses the issue of decision making and the resultant gain or loss. The poem is both the experience and the place. The inability or reluctance of the victim to express emotion could also be addressed through the popular song recorded by Melissa Manchester, "Don't Cry Out Loud" (Allen and Sager, 1976). The song speaks to the pain of hiding one's feelings. An exploration of the victim's reaction is necessary because it is possible for her to construe these lines as advocating that she control her feelings. The battered woman is often reluctant to share information openly in a therapeutic setting, as she has learned to try to resolve problems on her own and to protect the batterer. Poetry offers a way for the victim to express herself while at the same time maintaining control over what to keep to herself and what to share.

Expression of anger

Poetry can provide the structure for battered women to express the anger and rage that they have contained in order to protect themselves and their children. Langston Hughes' (1951/1970) poem "Harlem" could offer the opportunity for the battered woman to discuss her own personal experiences and perhaps identify what keeps her from "exploding". Or, if a battered woman has fought back, the poem could become a springboard to a discussion of the feelings and events leading to her present circumstance. The following stanza is from "Raggedy Ann Takes a Stand" (Grayson, 1985):

> *After 18 years of*
> *Belittling and battering,*
> *Of hiding in closets*
> *And behind locked doors,*
> *She stood in death-silent defiance*
> *Serving him divorce papers,*
> *Her diamond shining shameless*
> *Like the blade of a shrewd stiletto.*

The reference to the stiletto is, of course, symbolic. This poem shows a victim taking a constructive and seemingly successful new action to combat the abuse and affirm herself. In some situations, the battered woman, feeling trapped, threatened, and overwhelmed, resorts to killing (Browne, 1987).

Dissociation or splitting

In order to cope with the overwhelming pain of being abused, many women report a mind and body split whereby they separate the pain from the beating while the battering is occurring. This fragmentation is a defense mechanism that sometimes helps the victim to survive; however, it is important for the therapist to support the victim while helping her to gain self-control and integrate her mind and body. David Loggins' (1974) song "So You Couldn't Get to Me" expresses, through images of an island and a room, the need to get away from a hurtful partner. The song could assist the therapist in making a crucial connection with the victim's experiences and perhaps, through the use of a creative writing exercise, help the victim to recognize the pain and begin the rebuilding integrative process.

Denial or minimization

This defense mechanism allows the victim to endure the abuse and cope with the ensuing depression, but it reduces the victim's self-esteem. The denial also encourages the hope that somehow the batterer will change and the honeymoon phase will return. Asking the victim to keep a log or journal will provide a measure of reality that can be useful in a therapeutic situation. Employing sentence stems such as "I used to be..., but now I'm..." can also be a valuable technique to help instill hope and a vision (Koch, 1970, p. 156).

Compliance and willingness to please

Compliance and an attempt to please people in authority positions are other common behaviors employed by battered women to try to prevent violent episodes. This general compliance also includes rescuing behavior (e.g., covering up for him). Nikki Giovanni's (1980) poem "Woman" refers to a series of efforts on the part of the woman to engage her partner (lover). The poem concludes with the woman's affirmation of her own decision making.

Comment

The focus of this chapter has been limited to a consideration of poetry and battered women. However, even though the number of reported victims is much smaller and the physical harm less severe, a serious problem exists for male victims of spouse abuse, as well. Also, the problems of mutually combative partners and gay/lesbian battering have not been addressed in this chapter. The perspectives and problems of the abuser warrant attention if we are to understand fully the dynamics of the abuse. An examination of literary works, particularly the poetry and music that children and adults are exposed to and create, may offer some of the most powerful research available to understand and reduce family violence. Poetry offers a perspective and a promise in a journey toward peace in and outside of the home.

chapter eight

Poetry therapy
and the elderly*

Understanding the needs of the aging and their families requires a measure of emotional depth that is not often found in traditional methods of clinical practice. This chapter will focus on the subjective experience of the elderly as reflected in language, symbol, and story.

Schlossberg (1990, p. 7) noted that aging should be considered with respect to functional age rather than chronological age: "How well does the person love, work, and play?" Although the elderly as a whole are being grouped together in this chapter with respect to common issues, it is critical to recognize that they (as with other developmental groups previously mentioned) are not a clearly definable single group. Adding to the biological, psychological, and sociological theories of aging, this chapter is a contribution to an understanding of the aged through the poetic.

The place of poetry in working with the elderly in a variety of educational and helping capacities has been established in the professional literature. Getzel (1983) examined the role of poetry writing groups in social group work with the elderly. Silvermarie (1988) found that oral poetry composition by frail elderly residents in a nursing home helped increase friendship formation and reduced institutional loneliness and isolation. Numerous other writers have addressed the positive role of incorporating poetry reading and/or writing within programs for the elderly (e.g., Coberly et al., 1984; Kaminsky, 1974; Koch, 1977; Mazza, 1988b; O'Dell, 1984; Peck, 1989; Reiter, 1994; Saunders, 1983).

This time of life can be a uniquely creative one for the elderly. Poetry can assist the elderly in transcending loss and maintaining a vital connection to the life process and can provide a significant contribution toward interpersonal and intergenerational linkages.

---

* An earlier version of this chapter was published in Mazza, N. (1998) *Journal of Aging and Identity*, 3(1), New York: Human Sciences Press.

Poetic perspectives

This section will identify and discuss several popular poems relating to the elderly and their families. The selection is intended only as a starting point for those who choose to incorporate poetry in their clinical practice and education.

Loss

Losses relating to physical and mental abilities as well as relationships and the respect of others often negatively impact an elderly person's self-concept (Myers, 1989). Marge Piercy's (1985) poem "Does the Light Fail Us, or Do We Fail the Light?" captures the pain and rage of the narrator's father who is in a nursing home suffering from dementia. In "Alzheimer's: The Wife", C.K. Williams (1987) evokes the pain of a husband watching his wife deteriorate.

Lucille Clifton's (1987) poem "Miss Rosie" deals with a homeless woman who has lost everything, including her identity. The poet, however, affirms the woman's presence. In essence, the poet draws our attention to an aging, homeless woman through imagery and narrative. In clinical education and supervision, this poem could serve as an excellent springboard to discuss attitudes toward the aged and homeless. Each person carries a personal history. Are we interested in some histories more than others? How is the significance of each aging person determined?

Transition

Following are poems that address adaptation and transition issues for the elderly. Nikki Giovanni's (1972) "Legacies" relates some of the fears and difficulties involved in intergenerational communication. In this poem, a grandmother wants to teach her granddaughter how to bake rolls. The granddaughter is resistant to learning how because she fears a certain loss. The narrator concludes with a comment about how neither of them was able to say explicitly what they really felt. Death, loss, and the theme of unspoken feelings is also reflected poetically in several popular songs, most notably Mike and the Mechanics' "The Living Years" (Rutherford and Robertson, 1988).

Facing death may be the ultimate transition that could evoke a range of feelings from rage to acceptance; consider the following perspectives. Dylan Thomas' (1952) "Do Not Go Gentle into that Good Night" implores the aged person to fight for every last bit of life. Theodore Roethke's (1948) "The Waking" uses the context of a journey to evoke a feeling of resolution toward aging and death. The poem also serves as a lesson for future generations. William Carlos Williams' (1939) "The Last Words of My English Grandmother" evokes both rage and resolution. This poem portrays the final act of an ill grandmother who at first rages against being taken away by ambulance to a hospital. In a short time, she looks out the window and indicates a tiredness in both the view and life. It appears that the grandmother has expressed being finished with life and is ready to move on. However, there certainly are many possible interpretations of this poem. Many families struggle with convincing an elderly relative to seek medical treatment in a hospital, and this poem could serve to raise a number of issues relating to caregiving (e.g., guilt, powerlessness, despair).

Life and death as a journey is evoked as a positive experience by Ralph Waldo Emerson in "Terminus":

> *It is time to be old...*
> *Right onward drive unharmed;*
> *The port, well worth the cruise, is near,*
> *And every wave is charmed.*

In this poem, the 19th century scholar offered a philosophy as well as an image that could allow respondents in an educational setting to explore their own views on life and death and relate to the ship metaphor. Before any helping professional can be of assistance to the elderly, he or she must first examine personal viewpoints (philosophy). This poem can offer a start in that direction for the journey of the helper.

In "An Angry Old Man", James Kavanaugh (1977) portrays the despair that turns to anger for a lonely, old man. Inviting us to look beyond the hostile behavior, Kavanaugh speaks to the needs of this person to be recognized: "...Perhaps I will snarl back at him tonight/ To let him know he has been heard. ..." This poem could be introduced as part of a lecture on recognizing and understanding the hostile behavior of some elderly clients. The danger, however, in using this poem without discussion is that some helping professionals might conclude that all one really needs to do is snap back at hostile elderly people. In using poetry with clients or students, the importance of processing must always be maintained.

The couple/marital relationship

The power of a loving relationship as a sustaining life force with intergenerational impact can be found in the poems that follow. "Bean Eaters", by Gwendolyn Brooks (1963), is a poem about an elderly couple who have little in the way of financial resources; however, they find satisfaction and inner peace in their day-to-day activities. Their memories that are touched off by objects around them (e.g., a vase, an old receipt) prove to be of immeasurable worth that speaks to the therapeutic aspects of reminiscence.

The couple's memories appear to serve as an integrative device that allows them to connect past, present, and future. This poem addresses the power of the relationship, as well as the pain when an elderly couple is separated by death or circumstance (e.g., one partner in a hospital). Kathy Mattea's song "Where've You Been?" (Vezner and Henry, 1989) poetically traces a couple's relationship from courtship to old age. The partners, married for 60 years, are now in different floors of a hospital.

Alice Walker's (1968) "Medicine" evokes the therapeutic power of her grandmother lying beside her ill grandfather. On one level, the grandmother is there to provide medicine should the grandfather need it to ease his pain. On a more significant level, though, the real medicine is the marital relationship. When this poem is used in an educational capacity, many issues could be raised, including the importance of maintaining relationships when elderly persons are hospitalized or placed in a nursing home. The poem could also be used to discuss the importance of linking psychosocial services to medical treatment.

In addition to speaking to the marital relationship, "Medicine" is also a reminder of the impact such relationships have on children and grandchildren. Indeed, all of the helping professionals receiving (or providing) education and training will in some way relate to their own experiences pertaining to an elderly parent or grandparent. An excellent source for poetic material that relates to intergenerational messages is popular music. There are powerful lyrics in such songs as Harry Chapin's "Cat's in the Cradle" (Chapin and Chapin, 1974), which deals with a father/son relationship; Patty Loveless' "How Can I Help You Say Goodbye?" (Collins and Taylor-Good, 1993), which deals with life-cycle issues from a mother/daughter perspective; and Collin Raye's "Love, Me" (Ewing and Barnes, 1991), a song about a 15-year-old boy's recollection of his grandfather's loving story of his wife through their life and her death.

Voices of the aged

Poetry written by the elderly in community or institutional settings (e.g., newsletters) is another source that can be used in practice, education, and training. In *I Never Told Anybody: Teaching Poetry Writing in a Nursing Home*, Koch (1977) offers a number of structured tasks that he and Farrell used in a nursing home. For example: (1) think of the place you were born and write about what you remember; (2) think of your favorite color and write about it; and (3) write about a quiet time. The following are some excerpts from resident poems:*

---

* From Koch, K. (1977) *I Never Told Anybody: Teaching Poetry in a Nursing Home*, New York: Random House, pp. 72–74, 201. With permission of the author.

- *Quiet:* "The quietest time I ever remember in my life/Was when they took off my leg" (by Sam Rainey). "The quietest thing in my life was after plowing acres of corn" (by William Rosa).
- *Getting Older:* "I don't mind getting older/But I don't want to get any sicker/.../ I don't mind getting older/When people include me in their lives" (by Margaret Whittaker).

Peck (1989) also developed poetry workshops in nursing homes, and much of the poetry is collected in *From Deep Within: Poetry Workshops in Nursing Homes.* The following are excerpts of poems written on friendship:[*]

> *Friends are a rock*
> *Upon whom the storms of our lives beat.*
> —Dorothy
>
> *A special friend of mine passed away recently; ...*
> *I shall never forget all the goodness*
> *I got from her.*
> —Anna

Kaminsky (1974), one of the pioneers in bringing poetry writing programs to the aged, described his methods and experiences through narrative and offered a collection of the poems written by the elderly. Consider the following from "Old Age Home":[**]

> *In the past some cultures put out their old*
> *To be devoured by wild animals or die of starvation.*
> *We are more civilized, so*
> *Let them die of loneliness.*
> *I want to believe that life has meaning, so*
> *I must look for beauty.*

Saunders (1983) utilized poetry at an extended care facility. Similar to the above authors, she worked in an educational capacity. There is no question, however, that there were many therapeutic aspects. The following are some excerpts from her "students":[***]

---

[*] From Peck, C.F. (1989) *From Deep Within: Poetry Workshops in Nursing Homes*, New York: Haworth Press, p. 140. With permission.

[**] From Kaminsky, M. (1974) *What's Inside You, It Shines Out of You*, New York: Horizon Press, p. 220. With permission of the author.

[***] From Saunders, K. (1983) *Gift of the Strangers (Creativity: A Force for Change)*, Hancock, WI: Pearl-Win, pp. 49, 93. With permission of the author.

The Candle in the Face of a Child
A little girl was praying by a lit candle.
She's kneeling, her face all aglow
Just like a candle...
Tomorrow will come soon
And so will the night
And I'll always remember the girl praying
In the night.
—Cleone

The Little Gold Box
This little gold box used to contain matches.
You can still feel its scratches on the side.
It lit candles for fancy romances...
Memories are now stored.
When I hold my little gold box
I begin to think of many memories
That could be told.
—Minnie

In sum, the original poetry of the elderly written as part of an educational or therapeutic project, although not necessarily of the highest literary quality, could prove to be the most powerful in the education and training of helping professionals.

Application

Reiter (1994), combining receptive/prescriptive, expressive/creative, and symbolic/ceremonial modes of poetry therapy with the frail elderly, demonstrated how the introduction of a preexisting poem, "Rough Weather Makes Good Timber" by Lee Edwin Kiser, could break through the resistance of an 86-year-old, depressed, homebound widow with numerous physical ailments. The poem seemed to promote self-expression through personal stories. Reiter recorded the stories, condensed them into narrative poems, and presented them to the client. The poetic interventions proved to have a powerful emotional impact and provided some validations to the client's feelings and experiences. Reiter prescribed a poem to deal with the client's difficult situation (widow in failing health and isolated) that provided an element of hope. This led to the symbolic storytelling and creative modes of poetry therapy that enhanced the quality of life for this individual. As Reiter noted, "The elderly are keepers of thousands of stories and unwritten poems."

In addition to listening for the stories from the elderly, it is also useful to assess the poetic experiences of the elderly. Recalling the poetry the elderly may be familiar with from their earlier years (e.g., "Barbara Fritchie", "Man With the Hoe", "Invictus") could serve to validate the poetic approach and provide a means to build a relationship with elderly clients. In response to the introduction of "Hope Is the Thing With Feathers" by Emily Dickinson, the following two collaborative poems were created by a group of elderly patients in a long-term care facility (Mazza, 1988b, p. 83):

Sometimes
Sometimes
I bow my head
And fold my hands together.
I ask for inner strength
To make my sadness secondary
And pray more.
Sometimes
I look for something else to do
To go out
And think of happy days
That are many,
Or read a good book.
And sometimes
I don't have much to say.
And I know thinking is good.
There is a need to get myself together.

In this poem the patients look to their inner resources, including religion and memories. They also realize there are days when they have silence, and this is validated as being acceptable.

Hope
Hope is seeing my granddaughter visit me
And being proud of my mother,
Being able to walk
And do the things I can't do;
It is in my youth
And showing light;
In my husband's understanding.
It's hard to explain
You have to feel it.

The patients in this poem look to their families, both past and present, as sources of support. Hope is defined in terms of family and religion and by using the image of light. The poem also demonstrates that each person is aware of his or her physical self and recognizes the limitations but still has a desire to be productive. The last lines again point to times when words are simply inadequate and we rely on feelings and unspoken words.

The poems were essentially a vehicle for self-expression that provided psychosocial support and facilitated feelings of self-worth. Some of the collaborative poems were published in the hospital newsletter, enhancing the patients' self-esteem and providing a symbolic/ceremonial experience.

Silvermarie (1988) combined expressive/creative and symbolic/ceremonial modes of poetry therapy in her group work with frail elderly residents in a nursing home. She encouraged the residents to create poems orally, and she would write down the lines. In sequential fashion, group members were asked to provide a few lines about a specific memory. She would read back the poems of each member to the group and affirm the poetic elements. Silvermarie added the symbolic/ceremonial element through the use of ritual. To deal with physical limitations (e.g., hearing, memory, or visual impairment), name placards for each member were used in the sessions. Silvermarie also made it a point to stand behind the group member as she read his or her poem. This ritual affirmed the authorship of the poem and provided a visual cue to group members regarding whose poem was being read. Of particular ceremonial importance, at the beginning of each session a candle was lit, suggesting the experience was akin to special events or holidays. The lit candle promoted reflection, and the blowing out of the candle at the end of the session provided an element of closure and affirmation.

Davis-Berman and Berman (1998) advanced a "Lifestories Group" at a retirement facility that is consistent with the symbolic/ceremonial mode of poetry therapy. Building on the work of McAdams (1993) and White and Epston (1990), the authors noted the key role that stories and storytelling can have on the individual's life. The group consisted of eight members, ranging in age from 77 to 86, who were living independently. The group was structured into three phases (Davis-Berman and Berman, 1998, p. 7): "Phase one involved the telling of the story. Phase two asked respondents to teach some aspect of their dominant stories, while phase three involved doing things and activities related to the stories." The authors appeared to have addressed and linked the cognitive, affective, and behavioral domains of group members. Group members shared various experiences with meeting personal challenges. The members brought in personal items related to their stories to share with members. Soon, specific themes emerged in the group, most notably loss and death. The group process included attending to personalized meanings of experiences and led to developing new stories.

Comment

There are, of course, a number of factors that must be considered before using poetry therapy with the elderly. These include the client's history, ability to deal with strong emotions, previous conceptions about literature, physical limitations, and current environment. It appears, however, that once the elderly are given the opportunity to experience the poetic, the enthusiasm and commitment of the clinician can help set the conditions to promote healing and or increased quality of life. Overall, the poetic approach to clinical practice views the elderly as participants rather than exclusively recipients in the therapeutic process.

part four

---

*Research and
professional development*

chapter nine

Advancing the research base for poetry therapy: an agenda for the millennium[*]

The purpose of this chapter is to examine and develop the research base for poetry therapy. As noted in Chapter one, poetry therapy is defined as the use of the language arts in therapeutic capacities. The purview of poetry therapy includes bibliotherapy, narrative, and metaphor. For the purposes of research, terminology remains a problem due, in part, to its interdisciplinary base and differential use. Such related terms as "reading therapy", "literatherapy", "journal therapy", "scriptotherapy", and "narrative therapy" can all be found in the literature. The terms "interactive bibliotherapy" (Hynes and Hynes-Berry, 1986) and "poetry therapy" (Leedy, 1985; Lerner, 1978) are, for the most part, synonymous.

In an effort to contribute to the research base of poetry therapy, the three modes of poetry therapy will be examined: (1) receptive/prescriptive, (2) expressive/creative, and (3) symbolic/ceremonial. Multiple aspects of poetry therapy have been explored, including its role as an adjunctive technique, method of practice, theoretical framework, and philosophy of practice. A poetry therapy practice research model that addresses multiple uses is the most consistent with the state-of-the-art and contemporary psychological practice.

Bergin and Garfield (1994, p. 821), in their summation of the contributions made by the distinguished scholars writing in the *Handbook of Psychotherapy and Behavior Change*, stated that we are in an "age of eclecticism and empiricism" and an "atheoretical era". The authors

---

[*] Sections of this chapter were previously published by Elsevier Science in Mazza, N. (1993) Toward a research agenda for the 1990s, *Arts and Psychotherapy*, 14(1).

identified three traditional views on clinical practice: (1) social learning theory, (2) humanistic phenomenological perspective, and (3) social psychology with specific reference to catharsis and rituals. Bergin and Garfield noted that all of the views have merit; however, there is no single approach that can account for all of psychotherapy treatment effectiveness. Looking at contemporary views, three perspectives are again identified in Bergin and Garfield. One perspective involves a type of technical eclecticism that combines techniques focusing on facilitating the expression of affect, developing cognitive mastery, and promoting behavioral regulation. The problem noted in this model is the lack of empirical evidence for specific combinations or integrations of the techniques. So it is with poetry therapy. There are specific modes and techniques — for example, cognitive bibliotherapy for depressed older adults (Landrevelle and Bissonnette, 1997) and written emotional expression in improving health outcomes with respect to trauma (Pennebaker et al., 1997) — that have proven effective individually but not in combination.

A second contemporary perspective identified by Bergin and Garfield (1994) was a "generic" model involving formal, technical, interpersonal, clinical, and temporal aspects. This model was based on a statistical analysis of the elements of the model with respect to process and outcome. The conceptual framework is worthy of consideration for poetry therapy; however, given the artistic/scientific assumptions of most models of poetry therapy and the paucity of quantitative studies, the rigid quantitative analysis for clinical decisions would be problematic.

The third perspective was social cognitive theory, advanced by Bandura in 1986. This perspective builds on social psychology and cognitive/behavioral traditions. Cognitive restructuring is central to the therapies in this perspective. The therapeutic relationship and social control are also identified as key principles in promoting positive change within therapy with long-lasting effects beyond therapy. Most forms of poetry therapy could easily be considered within the above perspective which calls for multiple research methods and measures. Fortunately, poetry therapy is being researched in a time when, according to Bergin and Garfield (1994, p. 826), there is "a renewed emphasis on clinical significance of results." They also note there is a new emphasis on process research that complements outcome research. This is especially important, as differential uses of poetry therapy techniques are applied to family and group modalities.

Especially encouraging is the growing acceptance of narrative, qualitative, and ethnographic studies of psychological methods. These approaches can serve to advance the study of the artistic elements of poetry therapy while still building on the scientific (largely quantitative) studies. Bergin and Garfield (1994, p. 828) offered a balanced approach to clinical research in stating that "an objective approach to subjective phenomena can be addressed qualitatively and descriptively using rigor and, in many cases, quantification." Aldridge (1994) advocated single-case research designs for the creative art therapist as a way to study both process and outcome with appropriate levels of rigor.

Sue, Zane, and Young (1994) studied research on psychotherapy with ethnic minorities and identified some key issues, including types of research questions asked, selection of measures, and the role of culture. Poetry therapy practice and research are both part of a process of discovery and need not be separate domains. Heineman (1981) and Witkin (1989) advocated a heuristic paradigm that offers an alternative to and complements traditional experimental designs. Tyson (1992) noted that the heuristic paradigm is a philosophy of science and includes cultural, cognitive, and linguistic studies. Considering the interdisciplinary base of poetry therapy and the concern with language, feelings, expression, and communication, this is a paradigm worth exploring. It also appears to be consistent with the philosophical base of poetry therapy which draws upon the strengths of cultural diversity and is gender sensitive.

In short, the context and purpose of the research method must take precedence over debates on the superiority of one research method over another. General research questions being asked about most psychological models can be asked of poetry therapy. For example, drawing from Koss and Butcher's (1986) questions regarding outcome research on brief psychotherapy, the following could also be asked of poetry therapy:

1. How does improvement produced by poetry therapy methods compare to that produced by other methods?
2. Is one poetry therapy approach superior to another?
3. What client characteristics are related to maximal outcome with poetry therapy methods?

Specificity and replication are central to research in poetry therapy. There is still not a uniform definition of poetry therapy, and the lack of a rigorous definition of the term "poetry" poses some obstacles in conducting research. The obstacles, however, are surmountable if we adhere to Paul's (1967, p. 111) specificity question: "What treatment, by whom, is most effective for this individual with that specific problem, under which set of circumstances?" For example, does the use of published poems (such as Robert Frost's "The Road Not Taken") by a registered poetry therapist reduce depression related to career indecision in the early stages of treatment? This example could be refined by specifying particular poems, the point at which the poem is introduced (how long into the session), and method of delivery (orally, printed, or both). Poetry therapy practice techniques must be presented with enough detail so that other practitioners can replicate them. An adequate description of the techniques must precede their evaluation. Creativity is not compromised by clarity. Rigor and discipline apply to both art and science. Recognizing the need for continued refinement and in consideration of the timing, appropriateness, purpose, and consistency with clinical theory, the following poetry therapy techniques will be discussed within their respective modes of poetry therapy — that is, receptive/prescriptive, expressive/creative, or symbolic/ ceremonial.

Receptive/prescriptive

Preexisting poems

Read a poem (and provide a printed copy) to an individual, family, or group (or have the clients read the poem) and invite reactions. Short stories and other forms of literature may also be used. Providing the lyrics of popular songs and playing an audiotape of the song is still another variation of the technique. In addition to investigating the effectiveness of the actual technique on the process and outcome of therapy, one of the most difficult issues confronting clinicians is the selection of literature. As noted in Chapter two, this issue has been raised by several authors.

One of the most common guidelines in poetry therapy has been the use of the isoprinciple advocated by Leedy (1969c). This principle requires matching the mood of a poem to the emotional state of the patient/client. For example, a poem with a sad tone but ending with hope would be used for the treatment of a depressed person. Luber (1976) noted that the isoprinciple rests on the assumption that the mood of both a patient and a poem can be identified with accuracy and consistency. In a study of 30 subjects consisting of mental health professionals, university English professors, and psychiatric patients, Luber tested this assumption. A semantic differential was used to identify the general mood (positive or negative) of ten poems. The results indicated that only two of the ten poems yielded any significant differences in group ratings. All other poems yielded no significant differences in ratings by the three groups. Luber (1976, p. 50) concluded that "poems can be classified by general mood (positive or negative) and that this identification is consistently made by a wide variety of raters or readers."

In a later study, Luber (1978, p. 212) investigated "the interaction between poetic mood and the mood or emotional state of participants in a poetry therapy group." The subjects consisted of ten patients at a partial hospitalization program in a psychiatric institute. The patients participated in a series of five experimental (poetry therapy) and five control (current events) groups. All the sessions were conducted over a 3-week period by the same therapist. The goal was to assess the effect the material had on the mood of the subjects by using a semantic differential on the materials and subjects.

The results (Luber, 1978, p. 213) indicated there were "no significant differences between the first and second mood ratings (prereading and postreading) for any group in either the experimental or control conditions. In addition, only one significant difference was discovered between pre-reading and postsession mood ratings, and that was in one of the control (current events) sessions." Luber's data challenge the premise of the isoprinciple. He found that there were no interactive effects between the mood of a patient and the mood of a poem. He further noted the lack of evidence that poetry is responsible for changing mood. This is contrary to earlier suggestions by Leedy (1969c). Luber stated that the practitioner using poetry in therapy must seek a rationale other than its effect on affect or mood. He further stated that, to use poetry on a theoretically sound basis in group therapy, it would be necessary to identify group mood.

Brown (1977/1978) found partial support for the isoprinciple by examining the relationship between response to emotion-oriented poetry and emotions, interests, and personal needs. He found that people are most responsive to poems expressing feelings that are within their range of personal experience. Brown (1977/1978, p. 88) stated: "The perceptiveness of the subjects appears to be related to his/her currently experienced emotion, rather than to any usual or typical emotional trait of the individual." The author also noted that, although there is a relationship between present mood and perceptiveness, individuals may project their own usual mood onto poems and thus see a mood in a poem that does not exist. He noted that both transitory and enduring emotional traits have an effect on an individual's response to poetry.

Brown's findings are in contrast to earlier work conducted by Eysenck (1940) in which aesthetic responses were found to be consistent with emotional and temperamental characteristics. Brown's study was significant in identifying some of the factors underlying the isoprinciple, specifically with respect to personality factors and poetic response. He identified the existence of a mood projection. The implication from this study is that a poem should be selected on the basis of matching poem mood to the client's currently experienced emotional state. This further implies that prestructuring sessions with poems would be contraindicated. Roosevelt (1982) also used a semantic differential to study the effects of "deep level" poems compared to "surface level" poems.

As noted earlier, Schloss (1976) conducted a survey of approximately 1400 therapists to examine the extent of poetry being used in therapy. The results were inconclusive; however, Schloss' work helped to identify some of the difficulties encountered in classifying poems.

Berry (1978) conducted one study to investigate what role people's reading and/or writing played in their coping abilities, and in another study he tried to determine whether it is possible to provide a set of objective means for the therapist to select poems for patients. In the first study, he found that individuals who enjoy reading might be more receptive to some form of literary therapy and that individuals with writing skills might be more amenable to a therapy that included some aspect of creative writing. In Berry's second study, 27 college students from an introductory psychology class served as subjects. Five poems were randomly selected from a list provided by a therapist who used poems in her sessions at a psychiatric institute. A questionnaire was administered to the subjects to determine: (1) how an interpretation was achieved — was it based on a particular line, stanza, title, or entire poem; (2) what feelings were evoked from each interpretation — happy, sad, or angry; and (3) based on a 5-point scale, how well liked the poem was. The results indicated that the entire poem was most important in producing an interpretation and evoking a subsequent feeling. Of the five poems given to the subjects, Frost's "Stopping by the Woods on a Snowy Evening" achieved the highest absolute preference rating. Berry (1978, p. 140) also found that "a poem's preference rating is strongly influenced by the number of feelings which the poem evokes in the reader."

Rolfs and Super (1988), in a descriptive study, identified the importance of the process of poetry selection and noted transference/countertransference issues. Through case examples, the authors noted the importance of considering all possible meanings of a poem. Specific practice guidelines for the selection of poems in group therapy were provided. The guidelines relate to therapeutic goal, anticipation of client responses, categorization, and the order of poems used. A number of research methodologies can be used to build on each guideline — for example, goal attainment scaling to determine to what degree each goal was met, the use of a semantic differential to examine therapist and client response to each poem, content analysis for the purpose of categorization of poems, and observational measures to examine the sequence of poems used.

Rossiter, Brown, and Gladding (1990) investigated the effect of poem selection on therapeutic process and outcome. Using a qualitative research design, the authors conducted an analysis of the poem/therapist/participant interaction. They found that literature is more than a catalyst in the therapeutic process; the success or failure of particular poems may depend on what the poems and therapists "ask" or on the clients themselves.

Hynes and Hynes-Berry (1986/1994) offered the most detailed criteria for the selection of poetic material in therapy. They also developed a detailed recording form to examine both the process and product of interactive bibliotherapy (poetry therapy). This form is useful for teaching, practice, and research. Hynes (1988, p. 57) noted that the "Bibliotherapy Dialogue" section of the form could be used to "build behavioral evidence of responses to specific literature and the resulting dialogue." It should prove to be a valuable tool in advancing the research base of poetry therapy.

Reiter (1997) surveyed her colleagues from the National Association for Poetry Therapy regarding their most often used poems in practice. The following 22 poems were most often selected:

1. "The Journey" by Mary Oliver
2. "Autobiography in Five Short Chapters" by Portia Nelson
3. "The Armful" by Robert Frost
4. "The Rubaiyat of Omar Khayyam"
5. "If I Should Cast Off This Tattered Coat" by Stephen Crane
6. "The Road Not Taken" by Robert Frost
7. "Self-Improvement Program" by Judith Viorst
8. "Variation on a Theme" by Denise Levertov
9. "The Man in the Glass" by Elton Evans
10. "I Knew This Kid" by James Kavanaugh
11. "Marks" by Linda Paston
12. "The Truth in 1963" by Edgar Allen Imhoff
13. "Talking to Grief" by Denise Levertov
14. "Message" by Carol Bernstern
15. "This Is Just to Say" by William Carlos Williams
16. "Impasse" by Langston Hughes
17. "I Can't Go On" by Dory Previn
18. "One Art" by Elizabeth Bishop
19. "Swineherd" by Eilean N. Chuilleannin
20. "I Wandered Lonely as a Cloud" by William Wordsworth
21. "A Ballad of Dreamland by Algemon" by Charles Swinburne
22. "The Summer Day" by Mary Oliver

The above list is the result of an informal study. Further work remains to be undertaken to classify and study the effects of specific poems.

Expressive/creative

The expressive/creative mode of poetry therapy includes a wide range of techniques and points to the overlap of practice and research. For example, Williams (1992) introduced two assessment methods to identify the belief systems of adult survivors of childhood sexual abuse: (1) the Williams-McPearl Belief Scale, a 31-item scale designed to measure beliefs about safety, trust, power, self-esteem, and intimacy; and (2) use of subjective writings (poetry and journal entries) for the survivors.

Williams (1992, p. 19) noted that the use of "the creative writing of survivors of sexual abuse reveals much otherwise hidden or repressed information about their abuses, self-concepts, and basic beliefs." Although it is difficult to isolate the variables that effect change in one's belief system and well-being, if the subjective method of writing can restore choice and one's voice, it seems to be a reasonable practice to use it as both a therapeutic technique and an assessment device. In the instance of creative writing, the intervention is also the measure. It is a special kind of measure that implies respect for the worth and dignity of the individual.

Creative writing

As noted previously, a number of studies have supported the therapeutic benefits of written emotional expressions (Smyth, 1998). The use of creative writing (poems, stories, diaries, or journals) can be helpful in both assessment and treatment. The writing may be free writing (any topic, any form) or prestructured (the use of sentence stems such as "When I am alone..."). Creative writing exercises have been used with individuals (White and Epston, 1990), families (Chavis, 1986), and groups (Wenz and McWhirter, 1990). There is a substantial research base on the use of written expression to improve mental and physical health (Pennebaker, 1992; Smyth, 1998).

Sharlin and Shenhar's (1986) research supports the diagnostic value of adolescent creative writing. The authors studied the poetry of two adolescents who committed suicide (89 poems) compared to the poetry of two nonsuicidal adolescents (64 poems). They used a word analysis for classification into semantic fields. They found significant differences between the suicide and control groups in the loaded words and the occurrence of two major foci: "death" and "bad situation". Although working with a rather small sample, the authors contributed to the development of another means to help predict suicide among adolescents. They constructed a model for guidance in the early detection of adolescent suicide.

Dyadic poems

This technique (Mazza and Prescott, 1981) was developed for couples. A relevant song or poem is shared with the couple, and then the couple is asked to develop a two-line statement or poem (each person contributing one line) about the meaning of the poem or song. The introduction of the poem or song is optional; the couple may simply create a dyadic poem about their relationship. The poem is useful for assessment purposes: (1) Were the lines complementary or contrasting? (2) Who went first? (3) How was the task approached by the couple? In addition to a content analysis of the poem, observational measures could be useful in studying process, particularly the nonverbal responses.

Collaborative poems

In this exercise, each member is invited to contribute one or more lines to the group poem. This is often done toward the end of a session and usually reflects the current mood or predominant theme of a group. It is also useful to type the group poem and give copies to each member at the following session. Some research indicates that the collaborative poem advances group cohesion (Golden, 1994; Mazza, 1981; Mazza and Prescott, 1981; Mazza and Price, 1985) and is reflective of the group developmental stage (Mazza and Price, 1985). Further research could incorporate a content analysis of the group poem. Observational measures may also be used to study the process of developing the collaborative poem.

Journal writing

Journals, diaries, or logs can range from unstructured to highly structured, depending upon purpose and client needs. Adams (1996) reported on 50 cases involving structured journal therapy assessments (clinical interview and self-report questionnaire method). The journals were used at an inpatient mental health facility. Based on positive results and specifics from the patients (e.g., desire for more writing techniques, guidance, direction), a self-paced workbook was developed (see *The Way of the Journal: A Journal Therapy Workbook for Healing*, by Kay Adams).

Symbolic/ceremonial: metaphors and imagery

Using poetic expressions, images, or symbols derived from the client's language and experiences can also be helpful in promoting change (Combs and Freedman, 1990; Goldstein, 1989). Self-monitoring procedures can be used in preliminary investigations; however, the measurement of private events such as cognitions and images remains a problem. Cimineron (1986, p. 36) noted that assessment procedures have not been developed to "test sophisticated hypotheses about the relationship among cognitions, imagery, and emotions and their functional significance in human behavior." This is an area that would warrant narrative research procedures. Shaw (1993) investigated the role of metaphor with respect to therapeutic interpretation in dynamic therapy. Becker (1993) evaluated the effectiveness of metaphoric states in increasing perseverance. Both studies yielded positive results for the use of metaphor in therapeutic capacities. This is an area, however, that warrants much more research.

Poetry therapy and group work

Early attempts at the empirical investigation of poetry therapy focused on group modalities. Edgar, Hazley, and Levit (1969) employed an experimental research design comparing poetry therapy to conventional therapy for hospitalized schizophrenic patients in a group setting. The authors planned to use pre- and post-psychological tests (Rorsach, WAIS, HTP, Bender, and psychological interview) with matched groups; however, due to discharges and home visits, the administration of post-tests was not possible. The authors noted that the experimental (poetry) group showed improvement on the basis that more patients were discharged and that more home visits were made than in the control group. The study, although flawed, helped to identify some of the methodological problems in evaluating poetry therapy. Edgar and Hazley (1969) attempted to validate poetry as a group therapy technique in a college counseling center. Overall, the aforementioned studies indicate that the authors were attempting to measure too broad a topic. Specific attention to particular variables that account for change and a careful consideration of the context in which the therapy is conducted would improve further studies.

Buck and Kramer (1974), in a qualitative analysis, explored the function of poetry as a part of the group process. They identified a "cumulative effect" in poetry group therapy. This refers to their observations about a connection of elements and themes that appeared in the writings of the group members. The procedures in the poetry therapy group model were gradually learned and used by the group members. Mazza and Prescott's (1981) qualitative report provided further support of Buck and Kramer's findings. Goldstein (1989) reported on how poetry can facilitate achievement of therapeutic goals consistent with interpersonal theory. Using a case study design, Goldstein found a relationship between poetry therapy and Yalom's (1985/1995) therapeutic factors.

In an experimental study of a poetry therapy group model combining the use of a preexisting poem and collaborative poem in group counseling, Mazza (1981) found that poetry therapy did advance group cohesion and self-discovery. Based on the trends of the Moos Group Environment Scale (Moos et al., 1974), it was further found by Mazza (1981, p. 123) that the poetry therapy model "has the potential to help establish the conditions for developmental growth and facilitate group process." Golden (1994) in a later study found that collaborative writing in poetry therapy groups advanced group cohesion.

Bondy et al. (1990) conducted an experimental study on the use of the personal life history book method in group treatment for foster children. The Achenbach Behavior Checklist was completed by foster parents for the treatment and control groups. Results indicated that behavior problems were significantly reduced following 12 to 16 weeks of treatment. Academic performance was also improved for the treatment group.

Rossiter and Brown (1988) conducted a study on 25 interactive bibliotherapy (poetry therapy) groups led by 17 different facilitators over a 10-yer period in an inpatient mental health facility. Questionnaires to evaluate the treatment were completed by senior staff (psychologists, social workers, nurses). The results indicated a positive evaluation with regard to the quality of interaction among patients. The authors also examined the differential effect of poetry therapy on the patients, noting that it was particularly beneficial to withdrawn patients and least helpful to those with limitations in cognitive functioning (those who were brain damaged or delusional or had a limited attention span). Mattes et al. (1986) reported on a pilot study that examined the differential benefits of art, poetry, and movement therapy at a psychiatric inpatient facility. The authors used multiple measures including the clinical interview (DSM-III diagnosis), human figure drawing, selected MMPI scales, the Embedded Figure Test, the Similarities and Block Design subtests from the WAIS, and the Conceptual Level Analogy Test (CLAT). Although the study had some major limitations (validity of the predictor variables, inability to isolate the use of the arts from other treatment variables), it was a significant step in advancing further research.

Evaluation of practice

Poetry therapy is now past the stage of good intentions and anecdotal reports. Accountability and legal and ethical standards require an evaluation of the practice of poetry therapy. It is imperative to maintain high standards of assessment and evaluation while maintaining sensitivity and rigor in research methodologies. Unless there is evidence that particular poetic interventions work with particular clients, problems, or situations, it will be difficult to gain increased acceptance in the professional arena. Case studies and single-system, ethnographic, and conventional experimental designs are all needed.

Research agenda

The following are 19 directions for research in poetry therapy as we enter the next millennium:

1. Formulation of research questions that address process and outcome in poetry therapy
2. Development of poetry therapy practice models that can be replicated and subjected to empirical evaluation

3. Use of a cross-sectional survey method to examine the use of literature and creative writing by selected helping professions in clinical practice — for example, using social workers randomly selected from the APA Membership Register as the unit for analysis

4. Encouraging partnerships among researchers in the creative arts therapies

5. Further development of new instruments and/or the adaptation of existing instruments for assessment and evaluation purposes in poetry therapy (for existing instruments, see Corcoran and Fischer, 1994; Hersen and Bellack, 1988)

6. Promotion of both experimental and qualitative/heuristic research (It should be noted that doctoral dissertations are one of the most overlooked sources for research findings. A "Dissertation Abstracts" column was instituted in the *Journal of Poetry Therapy* in 1987; since that time, 170 dissertations relating to poetry therapy have been abstracted.)

7. Investigation of patient/client characteristics with different forms of poetry therapy for patients/clients suffering from specific disorders

8. Exploration of the variability between different forms of poetry therapy and between particular stages of the specific treatment process

9. Research on the classification of poetry and other forms of literature for therapeutic purposes

10. Integration of a research approach with the practice of poetry therapy through case studies and single-system research designs

11. Development of research on the therapeutic aspects of reading

12. Promotion of literary analyses relating to poetry therapy

13. Promotion of cultural and linguistic studies related to poetry therapy

14. Development of research funding priorities

15. Exploration of public and private sources of support

16. Encourage paying special attention to socially responsive programs (at-risk children, AIDS, family violence)

17. Consideration of epistemological and value questions relating to poetry therapy (which has particular significance for women and minorities in that their experience has often been omitted or distorted in the clinical research literature)

18. Research to explore the specific experiences and perceptions of those who engage in creative writing for therapeutic purposes

19. Development of theory building through research activities and an integration of thought systems related to poetry therapy (including an integration of appropriate existing theories, such as

social, psychological, or literary, that can further solidify the base of poetry therapy practice)

The place of the artist-practitioner can merge with the scientist-practitioner if an understanding of research and scholarship is based on the premise that there are many ways of knowing. Art and science require discovery and discipline.

Chapter ten

Toward a field of poetry therapy

In the preceding chapter, it was noted that establishing a solid research base for poetry therapy is grounded, in part, in legal, ethical, and accountability issues. The continued contribution of poetry therapy to psychological methods will be largely determined by its scholarship. The quarterly *Journal of Poetry Therapy*, now in its twelfth year of publication, has been a significant force in meeting that requirement. This chapter will focus on additional elements to advance the field of poetry therapy, including professional organizations, standards for practice, professional collaboration, education, supervision, and the need for a vision.

Building on questions raised by Levick (1985) for creative arts therapists, the following questions should be raised regarding poetry therapy:

1. What are the current obstacles that keep poetry therapists from becoming visible members of the mental health profession, and what steps need to be taken to overcome these obstacles?
2. What are the unique contributions of poetry therapy to psychology?
3. What can be gained from the interface of poetry therapy and psychology?

Those involved with the use of poetry therapy in clinical practice have the opportunity to become visible members of the psychology profession through affiliation with Division 10 (Arts and Psychology) of the American Psychological Association. In addition, there are members of numerous other APA divisions who have practiced and written in the related areas of poetry therapy — most notably Division 32 (Humanistic Psychology), Division 39 (Psychoanalysis), and Division

29 (Psychotherapy). Some of the key articles cited by Levick are also drawn from perceptual psychology (Division 3); clinical psychology (Division 12); consulting psychology (Division 17); adult development and aging (Division 20); theoretical and philosophical psychology (Division 24); psychology of women (Division 35); children, youth, and family services (Division 37); health psychology (Division 38); family psychology (Division 43); and group psychology (Division 49).

In short, the poetic has surfaced in most fields of psychology. What is lacking is a bridge to connect interdisciplinary interests and findings. Further, a bridge for interdisciplinary work would be of mutual benefit to the arts and psychology. Lindauer (1995) encouraged psychologists who were interested in the arts to cross boundary lines and make presentations and submit papers in the arts and humanities. Psychologists also need to learn more about using databases not limited to psychology (e.g., PsycLit). Most importantly, we need to establish a dialogue between fields of psychology and the arts.

The interdisciplinary bridge for psychologists to cross has been present since 1981, with the formal incorporation of the National Association for Poetry Therapy (NAPT). This organization, which has approximately 400 members and was originally founded in 1969 as the Association for Poetry Therapy, is now a strong and viable organization with members from various disciplines, including medicine, nursing, psychology, social work, literature, education, library/information science, religion, counseling, marriage and family therapy, and others. Annual conventions held in various parts of the country have attracted both national and international interest. Recent convention themes of the NAPT are perhaps most revealing of the interdisciplinary interest and the close connection between "the word" and "healing":

- 1999, Charleston, SC: "At the Crossroads of Humanities and Healing: How Written, Spoken, and Performed Words Enrich the Human Story and Spirit"
- 1998, San Jose, CA: "To Tell Our Stories: Creating Connections to Self, Community, and the Environment"
- 1997, Cleveland, OH: "Writing Our Lives — Laughter, Loss, and Love: Using Language Arts for Professional Practice and Personal Growth"
- 1996, Columbus, OH: "Words for Life: Clinical and Educational Development in Applied Language Arts"

But, perhaps it was some of the earlier conference themes that helped NAPT come of age:

- 1984, New York, NY: "Poetry Therapy Through the Ages: From Childhood Through Old Age"

- 1985, Evanston, IL: "Humanizing Our Technological Society Through Poetry"

The National Association for Poetry Therapy has set standards for certification and registration, maintains strict adherence to its code of ethics, and offers and reviews educational and training programs.

The certified poetry therapist (CPT) can work independently in nonclinical settings, such as libraries, schools, nursing homes, and public groups, to promote health and well-being. Certified poetry therapists can work in a mental health setting but not as the primary therapist; they must work with a qualified mental health professional. The requirements for a CPT include a Bachelor's degree, plus a total of 440 hours of training divided into the following specific categories: (1) 200 hours of didactic study of poetry therapy, (2) 60 hours of peer experience, (3) 120 hours of poetry therapy experience, and (4) 60 hours of supervision.

Registered poetry therapists (RPTs) can work in clinical settings as long as they meet the eligibility requirements (e.g., licensing) established by the states in which they are conducting their practice. The requirements for RPTs include a Master's degree in a clinical field (such as psychology, social work, counseling) and a total of 975 hours of training divided into the following specific categories: (1) 250 hours of didactic study of poetry therapy, (2) 60 hours of peer experience, (3) 300 hours of poetry therapy experience, (4) 100 hours of supervision, (5) 165 hours of institution experience, and (6) 100 hours of other meritorious learning.

Ultimately, the pursuit of certification or registration in poetry therapy rests with the needs and interests of the clinician. The advancement of the credentialing process in poetry therapy has stimulated the development of education programs, criteria for approved supervisors, and monitoring procedures. The issue of education is one that requires a careful examination of how and at what level (undergraduate, graduate, doctoral) poetry therapy should be taught. Should content in poetry therapy be infused with other courses? What should the foundation course on poetry therapy look like? Mazza (1986) noted that introducing literary material into graduate classes on human development, family treatment, group treatment, and crisis intervention could enrich the content and facilitate the attainment of course objectives while serving as a model for incorporating poetry therapy in clinical practice. For example, introducing a poem and inviting discussion relating to a crisis intervention could demonstrate the subjective aspects of crisis. A group poem written by the students, in addition to demonstrating the subjective aspects, can also show the power of group process and the therapeutic elements of cohesion. Mazza (1998c, p. 73) also found that using writing assignments and including short stories in a family therapy class "facilitated language skills sensitive to the client's subjective life experiences and unique history."

Consistent with a narrative approach to practice and an appreciation of a client's "story" and its personalized meanings, the use of language arts methods in teaching family therapy serves as a model for clinical practice. Johnson (1993) proposed that a study of Kafka's "The Metamorphosis" could be helpful in teaching many of the ideas and concepts of structural family therapy. Patterson and van Meir (1996, p. 59) wrote that "using narrative, music, and art in teaching psychopathology can balance the scientific, objective style of the DSM-IV," and the authors provided a substantial list of stories that could be used. Blake (1998) developed a poetry therapy education model that addresses ethnic and gender issues of how the poetic can be integrated into a clinical curriculum.

A course on the theory and practice of poetry therapy should introduce students to its historical, theoretical, philosophical, and practical foundations. The course format could necessarily combine a didactic and experiential form, with a great deal of attention being given to skill-building exercises. The student/clinician must first be aware of personal reactions before using poetry in therapy; therefore, early on, students should become actively involved in selecting, reacting to, and discussing a wide range of literary material (receptive/prescriptive mode). Similarly, becoming actively involved in various writing exercises (cluster poem, collaborative poem, dyadic poem, journal) is necessary (expressive/creative mode). Attention to how metaphors and rituals are used in everyday life and clinical practice (symbolic/ceremonial mode) rounds out the three major modes of poetry therapy. Course objectives should include attention to the theory of poetry therapy; the method's place among other arts therapies; its principles and techniques; an evaluation of practice, legal, and ethical issues; and special populations.

Supervision in poetry therapy is not a subject that has received much attention in the professional literature. Calisch (1989) offered an eclectic model of supervision for art psychotherapists that can be applied in principle to poetry therapists. Consistent with a current move toward eclectic or integrative models of clinical practice, Calisch integrates psychodynamic, interpersonal, person-centered, and behavioral approaches. The psychodynamic component emphasizes transference-countertransference issues. The interpersonal component deals with here-and-now issues. The person-centered component encompasses support, empathy, and growth. The behavioral component focuses on goals, skill building, cognitive procedures, and self-observation. Supervision, however, must always be consistent with professional identity, theoretical orientation, level of development, and purpose. Some individuals might be interested only in learning specific poetry therapy techniques that are consistent with their theory and practice models; others might want to develop poetry therapy as a specialization area. Always, the dangers and limitations must be emphasized.

Related to the topic of supervision is the matter of who heals the healer. Gladding (1987, p. 101) noted the importance of self-renewal for the therapist and advocated a "check-out place" where therapists can "cultivate the metaphors and images of the present reality, the past ideals, and the future dreams." Mercer (1993), a psychiatric nurse, provided a personal perspective on the self-healing aspects of writing. Davis (1998), also a nurse, wrote about how "key images" surface through her work and writing. Iovino (1996), a pediatrician, demonstrated how her poetry aided in her own healing. Montgomery and Graham-Pole (1997, p. 103) wrote about how "a piece of journalized poetry written by a psychotherapist and cancer survivor and an oncologist…could draw clinician and client close to each other's understanding and experience through the subjective voice of each."

Personal example

The death of a pet can teach us valuable lessons on love and loss. In retrospect, I found that the three modes of poetry therapy were evident in my family's response to the death of our cat. I read Judith Viorst's (1971) *The Tenth Good Thing About Barney* to my children. We had a ceremony when we buried our cat that included the creation of a special marker for the gravesite. And each of us wrote a special note about our cat. Later, I wrote the following short story (Mazza, 1995a):

Sibling Ceremony

On Christmas morning, Robby was slowly opening his presents, measuring each moment. His mother wondered why her 5-year-old son wasn't tearing through the wrapping paper or bouncing his new basketball. His father was drinking coffee. Beth poked her brother and asked, "What's wrong?" Robby murmured, "Nothing." He kept staring at the Christmas tree and the nativity set with all the figurines in perfect order. Finally, he blurted, "Santa Claus isn't fair!" Silence was followed by his father's question, "What's wrong, Robby?" Same question. Same answer: "Nothing."

After opening his last present, a dinosaur puzzle, Robby walked to the kitchen cabinet and searched for a can of cat food. He found one in the back of the soup cans but was unable to open it. He couldn't ask his parents to open the can because they would look at him funny. After all, Tom died at Thanksgiving time and there's no cat to feed now. Beth's eyes trailed Robby. Her 10-year-old hands could both open a cat food can and hold her trembling brother. And they did. The children went to the spot in the backyard where Tom was buried. They placed a small blanket and some food there. Robby carried a piece of red ribbon from one of his presents and asked his sister to tie it around a branch that had been used as a burial marker. A special prayer was followed by a game of basketball.

Later, coming inside for supper, Beth and Robby saw that the garland from the Christmas tree was in shreds, scattered on the living room floor. There were no questions from anyone. Only half smiles. Pawprints from the heart leave an invisible trail.

A few years later, I found that writing another short story helped me cope with another, more devastating loss. This is where the "cat lesson" comes in (Mazza, 1995b):

Certain Peace

Katy wanted to write a Christmas story for the *Tallahassee Democrat*. She had read that certain stories would be published on Christmas Day. She remembered the words of a teacher who once said to her, "If you write from your heart, the words will come and they will be special." Katy thought that maybe if she wrote a story showing all the love in her heart that she received from her mom and dad, then her parents would see it in the newspaper and come back to each other. Then maybe her little brother wouldn't have to keep asking whether Santa and Mrs. Claus were getting divorced, or if Santa would know to which house (mom's or dad's) to deliver his toys.

Katy wrote a story about the death of Felix, the family cat. Felix died last year, 4 days before Christmas. She wrote about the special burial in the backyard and how the whole family held each other. She wrote about how her dad and mom showed her that amidst all the sadness it was good to talk about some of the silly times with Felix — like the times when Felix would paw the bows off Christmas presents, chase the bows around the house, and then hide them under the bed. She realized it was possible to cry and laugh at the same time. For no particular reason, she gave her little brother a hug.

The story was published on Christmas Day. The divorce became final in January. Although much had been broken in Katy's family, her story remained whole.

All forms of writing, especially journal writing, can be helpful to the clinician in reducing stress, providing an outlet for feelings, and gaining a sense of order during difficult times. In essence, poetry therapy can be a form of self-supervision.

Resource development

There are numerous resources that are available to those seeking material and wanting to network with other professionals involved in poetry therapy and the related arts therapies. According to the National Coalition of Arts Therapies Associations (NCATA, 1998), the NCATA was founded in 1979 and "is an alliance of professional associations dedicated to the advancement of the arts as therapeutic modalities. NCATA represents over 8000 individual members of six creative arts therapies associations. The creative arts therapies include art therapy, dance/movement therapy, drama therapy, music therapy, psychodrama, and poetry therapy."

The place of poetry therapy in psychology can also be developed through involvement with the Modern Language Association, the American Library Association, and of course all the related helping professions (e.g., NASW, ACA, and AAMFT). Advances in technology allow the use of the Internet to access such databases as the Literature and Medicine Database (http://endeavor.med.nyu.edu/lit-med-db/topview.html, an annotated bibliography of prose and poetry that is being used as a resource in the medical humanities. The Poetry Society of America (http://www.poetrysociety.org/) maintains a Web page with numerous links to literary resources. And, of course, the National Association for Poetry Therapy (http://www.poetrytherapy.org) provides a Web page with a number of useful links.

A vision

As we approach the year 2000 and beyond, poetry therapy is clearly an innovation in psychotherapy that has the potential to contribute to the restoration of the balance between the art and science of clinical practice. Poetry therapy involves a middle ground where literary and clinical boundaries are pushed. Literature contains elements of therapy; therapy contains elements of literature. There is a place for the differential use of poetry therapy, whether it is technique, method, or theory.

The field of poetry therapy will continue to be enriched by international involvements. Just a cursory review of the poetry therapy literature yields articles from England, Venezuela, Japan, Germany, Canada, South Africa, and Israel. Membership in the National Association for Poetry Therapy includes individuals from ten different countries. Multiculturalism should be central to poetry therapy. Lewis (1997, p. 226) called for "a continuing process toward greater awareness and connection with diversity of ethnicity within countries and with the international use of the arts in psychotherapy."

Gladding (1998) noted the transition that the creative arts in clinical practice have undergone. He identified five trends that are relevant for poetry therapy: (1) upgrading research, (2) strengthening educational standards, (3) molding clearer identities, (4) working toward interdisciplinary practice and research, and (5) promoting accessibility through the use of computers and technology, most notably Web sites.

Bevan and Kessel (1994, p. 507) offer a perspective consistent with the theme of this book: "If we psychologists can relax about who we are and seek to address the richness and complexity of such human lives, psychology may well become...one of the humanities as well as one of the sciences." It appears that, although the reading and writing of literature is a unique and solitary process, the healing qualities emerge from the recognition that we are not alone in our struggles. The greatest danger to the above process is complete withdrawal. The greatest hope for the resolution of problems is within the sharing and lending a vision of what we experience. Honesty in expression and behavior illuminates poetry therapy. When poetry, narratives, and symbols are created and shared, the human connection in personal therapeutic and social situations can be a powerful force for change. Let's keep the poetry alive in our professional practice as we pursue the poetic with those close to us in our personal lives. Poetry therapy taps an appreciation of our humanity and affirms the restoration of choice. And decision making, through heart and mind, is a part of poetry and therapy.

References

References

Abell, S.C. (1998) The use of poetry in play therapy: a logical integration, *The Arts in Psychotherapy*, 25, 45–49.

Adams, K. (1990) *Journal to the Self: 22 Paths to Personal Growth*, New York: Warner.

Adams, K. (1993) *The Way of the Journal: A Journal Therapy Workbook for Healing*, Lutherville, MD: Sidran Press.

Adams, K. (1996) The structured journal therapy assessment: a report on 50 cases, *Journal of Poetry Therapy*, 10, 77–106.

Adler, A. (1954) *Understanding Human Nature*, New York: Fawcett (W. Beran Wolfe, trans.; original work published 1927).

Aldington, R. (1963) New love, in Pratt, W., Ed., *The Imagist Poem*, New York: E.P. Dutton, p. 73.

Aldridge, D. (1994) Single-case research designs for the creative art therapist, *The Arts in Psychotherapy*, 21, 333–342.

Alissi, A.S. and Casper, M. (1985) Time as a factor in social groupwork, *Social Work with Groups*, 8, 3–16.

Allen, P. and Bayer-Sager, C. (1976) *Don't Cry Out Loud*, Irving Music/Unichappell/BMI.

Allport, G.F. (1942) *The Use of Personal Documents in Psychological Sciences*, New York: Social Science Research Council.

Ansbacher, H.L. and Ansbacher, R.R., Eds. (1956) *The Individual Psychology of Alfred Adler*, New York: Harper & Row.

Ansell, C. (1978/1994) Psychoanalysis and poetry, in Lerner, A., Ed., *Poetry in the Therapeutic Experience*, 2nd ed., St. Louis: MMB Music, pp. 12–23.

APA Division Information (1998) American Psychological Association Web site, http://www.apa.org/about/division.html.

Astrov, M., Ed. (1962) *American Indian Prose and Poetry: An Anthology*, New York: Capricorn.

Baker, S.B. and Taylor, J.G. (1998) Effects of career education interventions: a meta-analysis, *Career Development Quarterly*, 46, 376–385.

Baldwin, C. (1977) *One to One: Self-Understanding Through Journal Writing*, New York: M. Evans & Co.

Bandura, A. (1986) *Social Foundations of Thought and Action: A Social Cognitive Theory*, Englewood Cliffs, NJ: Prentice-Hall.

Barker, P. (1985) *Using Metaphors in Psychotherapy*, New York: Brunner/Mazel.

Barron, J. (1973) Poetry and therapeutic communication: nature and meaning of poetry, *Psychotherapy: Theory, Research, and Practice*, 11, 87–92.

Becker, L.E. (1993) The Effects of Metaphoric States on Perseverance, doctoral dissertation, California School of Professional Psychology-San Diego, *Dissertation Abstracts International*, 54, 4381B.

Becvar, D. and Becvar, R.J. (1993) Storytelling and family therapy, *American Journal of Family Therapy*, 21, 145–160.

Bergin, A.E. and Garfield, S.L. (1994) Overview, trends, and future issues, in Bergin, A.E. and Garfield, S.L., Eds., *Handbook of Psychotherapy and Behavior Change*, 4th ed., New York: Wiley, pp. 821–830.

Berry, F.M. (1978) Approaching poetry therapy from a scientific orientation, in Lerner, A., Ed., *Poetry in the Therapeutic Experience*, New York: Pergamon Press, pp. 127–142.

Bevan, W. and Kessel, F. (1994) Plain truths and home cooking: thoughts on the making and remaking of psychology, *American Psychologist*, 49, 505–509.

Birren, J.E. and Deutchman, D.E. (1991) *Guiding Autobiography Groups for Older Adults: Exploring the Fabric of Life*. Baltimore, MD: Johns Hopkins University Press.

Blake, M.E. (1998) Poetry as a Means of Communicating About Gender and Cultural Issues: A Model for Feminist Social Work Education, doctoral dissertation, Florida State University, *Dissertation Abstracts International*, 59, 3967A.

Blanton, S. (1960) *The Healing Power of Poetry Therapy*, New York: Crowell.

Blinderman, A.A. (1973) Shamans, witch doctors, medicine men and poetry, in Leedy, J.J., Ed., *Poetry the Healer*, Philadelphia: Lippincott, pp. 127–141.

Bondy, D., Davis, D., Hagen, S., Spiritos, A., Winnick, A., and Wright, C. (1990) Brief, focused preventive group psychotherapy: use of personal life history book method with groups of foster children, *Journal of Preventive Psychiatry and Allied Disciplines*, 4, 25–37.

Bowman, D.O. (1992) Poetry therapy in counseling the troubled adolescent, *Journal of Poetry Therapy*, 6, 27–34.

Brand, A.G. (1979) The uses of writing in psychotherapy, *Journal of Humanistic Psychology*, 19, 53–72.

Brand, A.G. (1980) *Therapy in Writing: A Psycho-Educational Enterprise*, Lexington, MA: Heath.

Brand, A.G. (1987) Writing as counseling, *Elementary School Guidance and Counseling*, 21, 266–275.

Brenner, C. (1974) *An Elementary Textbook of Psychoanalysis*, Garden City, NY: Doubleday.

Brogan, T.V.F. (1993) Verse and prose, in Preminger, A. and Brogan, T.V.G., Eds., *The New Princeton Encyclopedia of Poetry and Poetics*, Princeton, NJ: Princeton University Press, pp. 1346–1351.

Brooks, G. (1963) The bean eaters, in *Selected Poems*, New York: Harper & Row, p. 72.

Brown, D.H. (1977/1978) Poetry as a Counseling Tool: The Relationship Between Response to Emotion-Oriented Poetry and Emotions, Interests and Personal Needs, doctoral dissertation, Cornell University, *Dissertation Abstracts International*, 38, 4575A.

Browne, A. (1987) *When Battered Women Kill*, New York: Free Press.

Bruscia, K. (1988) Perspective: standards for clinical assessment in the arts therapies, *The Arts in Psychotherapy*, 15, 5–10.

Buck, L. and Kramer, A. (1974) Poetry as a means of group facilitation, *Journal of Humanistic Psychology*, 14, 57–71.

Budman, S.H., Ed. (1981) *Forms of Brief Therapy*, New York: Guilford.

Burnell, G.M. and Motelet, K.P. (1973) Correspondence therapy, *Archives of General Psychiatry*, 28, 728–731.

Calisch, A. (1989) Eclectic blending of theory in the supervision of art psycho-therapists, *The Arts in Psychotherapy*, 16, 37–43.

Cartwright, T. (1996) Poetry, therapy, letter-writing and the lived life. Comment on Maryhelen Snyder, Gonzalo Bacigalupe, and Alfred Lange, *Journal of Family Therapy*, 18, 389–395.

Cashman, T. and West, T. (1974) *Lifesong*, Sweet City Songs, Inc.

Chapin, H. (1978) *Flowers Are Red*, Five J's Songs (ASCAP)

Chapin, S. and Chapin, H. (1974) *Cat's in the Cradle*, Story Songs, Ltd. (ASCAP).

Chapman, T. (1983) *Behind the Wall*, SBK April Music, Inc./Purple Rabbit Music.

Chase, K. (1989) About collaborative poetry writing, *Journal of Poetry Therapy*, 3, 97–105.

Chavis, G.G. (1986) The use of poetry for clients dealing with family issues, *The Arts in Psychotherapy*, 13, 121–128.

Chavis, G.G., Ed. (1987a) *Family: Stories from the Interior*, St Paul, MN: Graywolf.

Chavis, G.G. (1987b) Poetry therapy in a women's growth group on the mother-daughter relationship, *Journal of Poetry Therapy*, 1, 67–76.

Ciminero, A.R. (1986) Behavioral assessment: an overview, in Ciminero, A.R., Calhoun, K.S., and Adams, H.E., Eds., *Handbook of Behavioral Assessment*, 2nd ed., New York: Wiley, pp. 3–11.

Clifton, L. (1969/1987) Miss Rosie, in *Good Woman: Poems and Memoirs 1969–1980*, Brockport, NY: BOA Editions, p. 19.

Clifton, L. (1983) *Everett Anderson's Goodbye*, New York: Henry Holt & Co.

Coberly, L.M., McCormick, J., and Updike, K. (1984) *Writers Have No Age: Creative Writing with Older Adults*, New York: Haworth Press.

Cohen, L. (1993) The therapeutic use of reading: a qualitative study, *Journal of Poetry Therapy*, 7, 73–83.

Cohen-Morales, P.J. (1989) Poetry as a therapeutic tool within an adolescent group setting, *Journal of Poetry Therapy*, 2, 155–160.

Collins, B.B. and Taylor-Good, K. (1993) *How Can I Help You Say Goodbye?*, Reynsong Publishing/Burton & Collins Publishing.

Combs, G. and Freedman, J. (1990) *Symbol, Story, and Ceremony: Using Metaphor in Individual and Family Therapy*, New York: Norton.

Corcoran, K. and Fischer, J. (1987) *Measures for Clinical Practice: A Sourcebook*, New York: Free Press.

Cornille, T.A. and Inger, C. (1992) The armor metaphor in marital and family therapy, *Journal of Family Psychotherapy*, 3(4), 27–42.

Costantino, G. and Malgady, R.G. (1986) *Cuento* therapy: a culturally sensitive modality for Puerto Rican children, *Journal of Consulting and Clinical Psychology*, 54, 639

Crane, S. (1970) If I should cast off this tattered coat, in Dore, A., Ed., *The Premier Book of Major Poets*, Greenwich, CT: Fawcett, p. 288 (original work published in 1895).

Creed, L. and Masser, M. (1977) *The Greatest Love of All*, Golden Torch Music Corp. and Gold Horizon Music Corp.

Crootof, C. (1969) Poetry therapy for psychoneutorics in a mental health center, in Leedy, J.J., Ed., *Poetry Therapy: The Use of Poetry in the Treatment of Emotional Disorders*, Philadelphia, PA: Lippincott, pp. 38–51.

Curran, J.M. (1989a) A family matter, *Journal of Poetry Therapy*, 2, 279.

Curran, J.M. (1989b) Just like dad, *Journal of Poetry Therapy*, 2, 278.

Davis, C. (1998) Touching creation's web: key images in poetry, *Journal of Poetry Therapy*, 11, 215–222.

Davis, E. (1977) *The Liberty Cap: A Catalogue of Non-Sexist Materials for Children*, Chicago: Academy Press.

Davis, M.S. (1979) Poetry therapy versus interpersonal group therapy: comparison of treatment effectiveness with depressed women, doctoral dissertation, The Wright Institute, *Dissertation Abstracts International*, 39, 5543B.

Davis, S.L. (1996) Poetry as hidden voice: adults with developmental disabilities speak out, *Journal of Poetry Therapy*, 9, 143–148.

Deats, S.M. and Lenker, L.T. (1989) *Youth Suicide Prevention: Lessons from Literature*, New York: Plenum Press.

Deats, S.M. and Lenker, L.T., Eds. (1991) *The Aching Hearth: Family Violence in Life and Literature*, New York: Plenum Press.

De Maria, M.B. (1991) Poetry and the abused child: the forest and the tinted plexiglass, *Journal of Poetry Therapy*, 5, 79–93.

Denver, J. (1975) *Looking for Space*, Cherry Lane Music.

Diana, N.M. (1998) Let me tell you a story...using fairy tales and fables with the hard to treat client, *Journal of Poetry Therapy*, 11, 175–181.

Díaz de Chumaceiro, C.L. (1996) Freud, poetry, and serendipitous parapraxes, *Journal of Poetry Therapy*, 10, 237–243.

Díaz de Chumaceiro, C.L. (1997) Unconsciously induced recall of prose and poetry: an analysis of manifest and latent contents, *Journal of Poetry Therapy*, 10, 237–243.

Díaz de Chumaceiro, C.L. (1998) Hamlet in Freud's thoughts: reinterpretations in the psychoanalytic literature, *Journal of Poetry Therapy*, 11, 139–153.

Dickinson, E. (1959) I'm nobody, in Linscott, R.N., Ed., *Selected Poems and Letters of Emily Dickinson*, New York: Doubleday, p. 73 (original work published in 1861).

Dickinson, E. (1961) Hope is the thing with feathers, in Johnson, T.H., Ed., *Final Harvest: Emily Dickinson's Poems*, Boston: Little, Brown, & Co., p. 63 (original work published in 1861).

Donnelly, D.A. and Murray, E.J. (1991) Cognitive and emotional charnges in written essays and therapy interviews, *Journal of Social and Clinical Psychology*, 10, 334–350.

Dore, A., Ed. (1970) *The Premier Book of Major Poets*, Greenwich, CT: Fawcett.

Drewery, W. and Winslade, J. (1997) The theoretical story of narrative therapy, in Monk, G., Winslade, J., Crocket, K., and Epston, D., Eds., *Narrative Therapy in Practice: The Archaeology of Hope*, San Francisco, CA: Jossey-Bass, pp. 32–52.

Dreyer, S.S. (1977) *The Bookfinder: A Guide to Children's Literature About the Needs and Problems of Youth Ages 2–15*, Circle Pines, MN: American Guidance Service.

Dreyer, S.S. (1992) *The Best of Bookfinder: A Guide to Children's Literature About Interests and Concerns of Youth Ages 2–18*, Circle Pines, MN: American Guidance Service.

Edgar, K.F. and Hazley, R. (1969) Validation of poetry as a group therapy technique, in Leedy, J.J., Ed., *Poetry Therapy*, Philadelphia, PA: Lippincott, pp. 111–123.

Edgar, K.F., Hazley, R. and Levit, H.L. (1969) Poetry therapy with hospitalized schizophrenics, in Leedy, J.J., Ed., *Poetry Therapy*, Philadelphia, PA: Lippincott, pp. 29–37.

Eliot, T.S. (1936) Preludes, in *T.S. Eliot Selected Poems*, New York: Harcourt, Brace & World, pp. 22–24.

Ellis, A. (1955) New approaches to psychotherapy techniques, *Journal of Clinical Psychology*, 11, 207–216.

Emerson, R.W. (1946) Terminus, in van Doren, M., Ed., *The Portable Emerson*, New York: Viking, pp. 346–347 (original work published in 19th century).

Erickson, M.H. and Rossi, E.L. (1980) Two-level communication and the microdynamics of trance and suggestion, in Rossi, E.L., Ed., *The Collected Papers of Milton H. Erickson on Hyponosis. Vol. 1. The Nature of Hyponosis and Suggestion*, New York: Irvington, pp. 430–451.

Erikson, E.H. (1968) *Identity, Youth, and Crisis*, New York: Norton.

Ewing, S. and Barnes, M.T. (1991) *Love, Me*, Acuff-Rose Music, BMI.

Eysenck, H.J. (1940) Some factors in the appreciation of poetry, and their relations to temperamental qualities, *Character and Personality*, 9, 161–167.

Farber, D.J. (1953) Written communication in psychotherapy, *Psychiatry*, 16, 365–374.

Ford, D. and Urban, H. (1963) *Systems of Psychotherapy*, New York: Wiley.

Forsey, K. (1983) *Lady, Lady, Lady*, Paramount Pictures.

Fowler, R.D. (1998) The healing arts, *APA Monitor*, 29(March), 3.

Fox, C. and Gimble, N. (1973) *I Got a Name*, Fox Fanfare Music.

Fox, R. (1982) The personal log: enriching clinical practice, *Clinical Social Work Journal*, 10, 94–102.

Francis, M.E. and Pennebaker, J.W. (1992) Putting stress into words: the impact of writing on physiological, absentee, and self-reported emotional well-being measures, *American Journal of Health Promotion*, 6, 280–287.

Frank, J.D. (1973) *Persuasion and Healing*, rev. ed., Baltimore, MD: Johns Hopkins University Press.

Freud, S. (1959) The relation of the poet to day-dreaming, in Riviere, J., trans., *Collected Papers of Sigmund Freud. Vol. 4*, New York: Basic Books (original work published 1908).

Friedman, E.H. (1990) *Friedman's Fables*, New York: Guilford.

Frost, R. (1915/1964) The road not taken, in *Complete Poems of Robert Frost*, New York: Holt, Rinehart, & Winston, p. 131 (original work published in 1915).

Gabriel, P. (1986) *Don't Give Up*, Cliofine LPDP/Hidden Pun Music, Inc. (BMI).

Garfield, S.L. and Bergin, A.E. (1994) Introduction and historical overview, in Bergin, A.E. and S.L. Garfield, S.L., Eds., *Handbook of Psychotherapy and Behavior Change*, 4th ed., New York: John Wiley & Sons, pp. 3–18.

Garland, J.A., Jones, J., and Kolodny, R. (1965) A model for stages of development in social work groups, in Bernstein, S., Ed., *Explorations in Group Work*, Boston: Boston University School of Social Work, pp. 12–53.

Gatz, Y. and Christie L. (1991) Marital group metaphors: significance in the life stages of group development, *Contemporary Family Therapy*, 13, 103–126.

Gendler, J.R. (1984/1988) *The Book of Qualities*, New York: Harper Perennial.

Gergen, K.J. (1994) *Realities and Relationships: Soundings in Social Construction*, Cambridge, MA: Harvard University Press.

Germain, C.B. (1976) Time: an ecological variable in social work practice, *Social Casework*, 57, 419–426.

Getzel, G.S. (1983) Poetry writing groups and the elderly: a reconsideration of art and social group work, *Social Work with Groups*, 6, 65–76.

Ghostwriter: Come to Your Senses (1993) New York: Children's Television Workshop.

Gibran, K. (1952) On marriage, in *The Prophet*, New York: Knopf, pp. 19–20.

Gil, G. (1979) *Here and Now*, Rondra Music, Inc.

Gillian, M.A. and Gillian, J., Eds. (1994) *Unsettling America: An Anthology of Contemporary Multiculturel Poetry*, New York: Penguin.

Ginzberg, E. (1972) Toward a theory of occupational choice: a restatement, *Vocational Guidance Quarterly*, 20, 169–176.

Ginzberg, E., Ginzberg, S.W., Axelrad, S. and Herma, J.L. (1951) *Occupational Choice: An Approach to General Theory*, New York: Columbia University Press.

Giovanni, N. (1972a) Legacies, in *My House: Poems by Nikki Giovanni*, New York: William Morrow, p. 5.

Giovanni, N. (1972b) The world is not a pleasant place to be, in *My House: Poems by Nikki Giovanni*, New York: William Morrow, p. 15.

Giovanni, N. (1976) Nikki Rosa, in Konek, C. and Walters, D., Eds., *I Hear My Sisters Saying: Poems by Twentieth Century Women*, New York: Crowell, pp. 8–9 (original work published in 1968).

Giovanni, N. (1980a) Masks, in *Vacation Time: Poems for Children*, New York: William Morrow, p. 53.

Giovanni, N. (1980b) Woman, in *Poems by Nikki Giovanni: Cotton Candy on a Rainy Day*, New York: William Morrow, p. 71.

Gladding, S.T. (1985) Family poems: a way of modifying family dynamics, *The Arts in Psychotherapy*, 12, 239–243.

Gladding, S.T. (1987) The poetics of a "check out" place: preventing burnout and promoting self-renewal, *Journal of Poetry Therapy*, 1, 95–102.

Gladding, S.T. (1998) *Counseling as an Art: The Creative Arts in Counseling*, 2nd ed., Alexandria, VA: American Counseling Association.

Gladding, S.T. and Heape, S.E. (1987) Popular music as a poetic metaphor in family therapy, *American Journal of Social Psychiatry*, 7, 109–111.

Gold, J. and Gloade, F. (1988) Affective reading and its life application, *The Arts in Psychotherapy*, 15, 235–244.

Goldberg, N. (1986) *Writing Down the Bones: Freeing the Writer Within*, Boston: Shambhala Publications.

Golden, K.M. (1994) The Effect of Collaborative Writing on Cohesion in Poetry Therapy Groups, doctoral dissertation, The American University, *Dissertation Abstracts International*, 56, 867–868A.

Goldstein, M. (1989) Poetry and therapeutic factors in group therapy, *Journal of Poetry Therapy*, 2, 231–241.

Gordon, D. (1978) *Therapeutic Metaphors: Helping Others Through the Looking Glass*, Cupertino, CA: Meta Publications.

Grayson, D.E. (1985) Raggedy Ann takes a stand, in Honton, M., Ed., *The Poet's Job: To Go Too Far*, Columbus, OH: Sophia Books.

Green, A.H. (1978) Psychopathology of abused children, *Journal of the Academy of Child Psychiatry*, 17, 92–103.

Griefer, E. (1963) *Principles of Poetry Therapy*, New York: Poetry Therapy Center.

Gumina, J.M. (1980) Sentence completion as an aid in sex therapy, *Journal of Marital and Family Therapy*, 62, 201–206.

Hall, C.S. and Lindzey, G. (1978) *Theories of Personality*, New York: Wiley.

Harrower, M. (1972) *The Therapy of Poetry*. Springfield, IL: Charles C Thomas.

Heineman, M.B. (1981) The obsolete scientific imperitive in social work research, *Social Service Review*, 55, 371–397.

Hersen, M. and Bellack, A.S., Eds. (1988) *Dictionary of Behavioral Assessment Techniques*, New York: Pergamon Press.

Hill, D. (1979) *Perfect Man*, If Dreams Had Wings Music, Ltd.

Hill, D. and Mann, B. (1977) *Sometimes When We Touch*, Welbeck Music (ASCAP)/ ATV Music (BMI).

Hillman, J.S. (1976) Occupational roles in children's literature, *The Elementary School Journal*, 77, 1–4.

Ho, M.K. and Settles, A. (1984) The use of popular music in family therapy, *Social Work*, 29, 65–67.

Hodas, G.R. (1991) Using original music to explore gender and sexuality with adolescents, *Journal of Poetry Therapy*, 4, 205–220.

Holman, W.D. (1996) The power of poetry: validating ethnic identity through a bibliotherapeutic intervention with a Puerto Rican adolescent, *Child and Adolescent Social Work Journal*, 13, 371–383.

Horowitz, L., Leffert, N., and DuBois-Schmitz, L. (1987) Collaborative poems on divorce, *Journal of Poetry Therapy*, 1, 61–62.

Hovda, P. (1977) Child welfare: child abuse, in Turner, J.B., Ed., *Encyclopedia of Social Work*, Vol. I, Washington, DC: NASW Press, pp. 125–129.

Hughes, L. (1970) Harlem, in Dore, A., Ed., *The Premier Book of Major Poets*, Greenwich, CT: Fawcett, p. 206 (original work published in 1951).

Hynes, A.M. (1987) Biblio/poetry therapy in women's shelters, *American Journal of Social Psychiatry*, 7, 112–116.

Hynes, A.M. (1988) Some considerations concerning assessment in poetry therapy and interactive bibliotherapy, *The Arts in Psychotherapy*, 15, 55–62.

Hynes, A.M. and Hynes-Berry, M. (1986/1994) *Biblio/Poetry Therapy — The Interactive Process: A Handbook*, St. Cloud, MN: North Star Press.

Hynes, A.M. and Hynes-Berry, M. (1992) *Biblio/Poetry Therapy: A Resource Bibliography*, St, Joseph, MN: The Bibliotherapy Roundtable.

Ian, J. (1974) *At Seventeen*, Mine Music, Ltd./April Music, Inc. (ASCAP).

Ignatow, D. (1964) Brooding, in *Figures of the Human*, Middleton, CT: Wesleyan University Press, p. 53.

Imber-Black, E., Roberts, J., and Whiting, R. (1988) *Rituals in Families and Family Therapy*, New York: W.W. Norton.

Iovino, R. (1996) Wounded healer: a physician's poetic perspective, *Journal of Poetry Therapy*, 10, 87–94.

Joel, B. (1973) *Piano Man*, Blackwood Music, Inc.

Joel, B. (1985) *You're Only Human*, Blackwood Music, Inc.

Johnson, D.R. (1986) Perspective: envisioning the link among the creative arts therapies, *The Arts in Psychotherapy*, 12, 233–238.

Johnson, S. (1991) Storytelling and the therapeutic process: the teller's trance, *Journal of Poetry Therapy*, 4, 141–148.

Johnson, S. (1993) Structural elements in Franz Kafka's "The Metamorphosis", *Journal of Marital and Family Therapy*, 19, 149–157.

Jones, R.E. (1969) Treatment of a psychotic patient by poetry therapy, in Leedy, J.J., Ed., *Poetry Therapy: The Use of Poetry in the Treatment of Emotional Disorders*, Philadelphia, PA: Lippincott, pp. 19–25.

Josefowitz, N. (1983) Can't do it all, in *Is This Where I Was Going? Verses for Women in the Midst of Life*, New York: Warner, p. 14.

Joseph, S.M., Ed. (1969) *The Me Nobody Knows: Children's Voices from the Ghetto*, New York: Avon.

Jung, C.G. (1972) On the relation of analytical psychology to poetry, in Campbell, J., Ed. (R.F.C. Hull, trans.), *The Portable Jung*, New York: Viking Press (original work published 1922).

Kaminsky, M. (1974) *What's Inside You, It Shines Out of You*, New York: Horizon.

Kaminsky, M. (1985) The arts and social work: writing and reminiscing in old age, *Journal of Gerontological Social Work*, 8, 225–246.

Kanfer, F.H. (1979) Self-management: strategies and tactics, in Goldstein, A.P. and Kanfer, F.H., Eds., *Maximizing Treatment Gains: Transfer Enhancement in Psychotherapy*, New York: Academic Press, p. 189.

Kavanaugh, J. (1977) An angry old man, in *Winter Has Lasted Too Long*, New York: E.P. Dutton.

Kempe, R.S. and Kempe, C.H. (1984) *The Common Secret: Sexual Abuse of Children and Adolescents*, New York: W.H. Freeman.

Kiell, N. (1990) *Psychoanalysis, Psychology, and Literature: A Bibliography*, Metuchen, NJ: Scarecrow Press.

King, C. (1972) *Bitter with the Sweet*, Colgems/CMI Music, Inc.

Kissman, K. (1989) Poetry and feminist social work, *Journal of Poetry Therapy*, 2, 221–230.

Kliman, G. (1990) *The Personal Life History Book: A Manual for Brief, Focused Preventive Psychotherapy with Foster Children. I. How To Do It. II. The Personal Life History Book, Child's Version*, Kentfield, CA: Psychological Trauma.

Knapp, J.V. (1996) *Striking at the Joints: Contemporary Psychology and Literary Criticism*, Lanham, MD: University Press of America.

Knell, S.,and Winer, G.A. (1979) Effects of reading content on occupational sex-role stereotypes, *Journal of Vocational Behavior*, 14, 78–87.

Koch, K. (1970) *Wishes, Lies, and Dreams: Teaching Children to Write Poetry*, New York: Harper & Row.

Koch, K. (1973) *Rose, Where Did You Get That Red?*, New York: Random House.

Koch, K. (1977) *I Never Told Anybody: Teaching Poetry Writing in a Nursing Home*, New York: Random House.

Konopka, G. (1966) *The Adolescent Girl in Conflict*, Englewood Cliffs, NJ: Prentice-Hall.

Konopka, G. (1983) Adolescent suicide, *Exceptional Children*, 49, 390–394.

Koss, M.P. and Butcher, J.N. (1986) Research on brief psychotherapy, in Garfield, S.L. and Bergin, A.E., Eds., *Handbook of Psychotherapy and Behavior Change*, 3rd ed., New York: Wiley, pp. 627–670.

Koss, M.P., Butcher, J.N., and Strupp, H.H. (1986) Brief psychotherapy methods in clinical research, *Journal of Consulting and Clinical Psychology*, 54, 60–67.

Kramer, A. (1990) Poetry and group process: restoring heart and mind, *Journal of Poetry Therapy*, 3, 221–227.

L'Abate, L. (1993) An application of programmed writing: arguing and fighting, in Nelson, T.S. and Trepper, T.S., Eds., *101 Interventions in Family Therapy*, New York: Haworth Press, pp. 350–354.

L'Abate, L. and Cook, J. (1992) *Programmed Writing: Self-Administered Approach for Intervention with Individuals, Couples, and Families*, Pacific Grove, CA: Brooks/Cole.

Lacour, C.B. (1993) Romantic and postromantic poetics, in Preminger, A. and Brogan, T.V.F., Eds., *The New Princeton Encyclopedia of Poetry and Poetics*, Princeton, NJ: Princeton University Press, pp. 1346–1351.

Landreville, P. and Bissonnette, L. (1997) Effects of cognitive bibliotherapy for depressed older adults with a disability, *Clinical Gerontologist*, 17, 35–55.

Landsman, T. (1951) The therapeutic use of written materials, *American Psychologist*, 6, 347.

Lange, A. (1994) Writing assignments in treatment of grief and traumas from the past, in Zerig, J., Ed., *Ericksonian Methods: The Essence of the Story*, New York: Brunner/Mazel, pp. 377–392.

Lankton, C.H. and Lankton, S.R. (1989) *Tales of Enchantment: Goal-Oriented Metaphors for Adults and Children in Therapy*, New York: Brunner/Mazel.

Lauer, R. and Goldfield, M. (1970) Creative writing in group therapy, *Psychotherapy: Theory, Research, and Practice*, 7(4), 248–252.

Leedy, J.J. (1969a) Introduction: the healing power of poetry, in Leedy, J.J., Ed., *Poetry Therapy: The Use of Poetry in the Treatment of Emotional Disorders*, Philadelphia, PA: Lippincott, pp. 11–13.

Leedy, J.J., Ed. (1969b) *Poetry Therapy: The Use of Poetry in the Treatment of Emotional Disorders*, Philadelphia, PA: Lippincott.

Leedy, J.J. (1969c) Principles of poetry therapy, in Leedy, J.J., Ed., *Poetry Therapy: The Use of Poetry in the Treatment of Emotional Disorders*, Philadelphia, PA: Lippincott, pp. 67–74.

Leedy, J.J. (1973) *Poetry the Healer*. Philadelphia, PA: Lippincott.

Leedy, J.J., Ed. (1985) *Poetry as Healer: Mending the Troubled Mind*, New York: Vanguard.

Leedy, J.J. and Rapp, E. (1973) Poetry therapy and some links to art therapy, *Art Psychotherapy*, 1(2), 145–151.

Leonard, G.E. (1971) Career guidance in the elementary school, *Elementary School Guidance and Counseling*, 6, 124–126.

Lerner, A. (1975) Poetry as therapy, *APA Monitor*, 6(4).

Lerner, A. (1976) Editorial: a look at poetry therapy, *Art Psychotherapy*, 3, i.

Lerner, A., Ed. (1978) *Poetry in the Therapeutic Experience*, New York: Pergamon Press.

Lerner, A. (1982) Poetry therapy in the group experience, in Abt, L.E. and Stuart, I.R., Eds., *The Newer Therapies: A Sourcebook*, New York: Van Nostrand-Reinhold, pp. 228–248.

Lerner, A. (1987) Poetry therapy corner, *Journal of Poetry Therapy*, 7, 54–56.

Lerner, A. (1992) Poetry therapy corner: the Poetry Therapy Institute (1973–1992), *Journal of Poetry Therapy*, 6, 107–110.

Lerner, A., Ed. (1994) *Poetry in the Therapeutic Experience*, 2nd ed., St. Louis, MO: MMB Music, Inc.

Lerner, A. and Mahlendorf, U.R., Eds. (1987) Poetry in therapy [special issue], *The American Journal of Social Psychiatry*, 7(2).

Lerner, A. and Mahlendorf, U.R., Eds. (1991) *Life Guidance through Literature*, Chicago, IL: American Library Association.

Lessner, J.W. (1974) The poem as catalyst in group counseling, *Personnel and Guidance Journal*, 53(1), 33–38.

Levick, M. (1985) Friday morning panel, in *Looking Ahead, Planning Together: The Creative Arts in Therapy as an Integral Part of Treatment for the '90s* (symposium proceedings), Philadelphia, PA: Hahnemann University.

Lewis, P. (1997) Appreciating diversity, commonality, and the transcendent through the arts therapies, *The Arts in Psychotherapy*, 24, 225–226.

Lindauer, M.S. (1995) Psychology, art, and a new look at interdisciplinarity: a personal view, *Psychology and the Arts*, Fall/Winter, 12–16.

Loggins, D. (1974) *So You Couldn't Get to Me*, Leeds Music Corp./Antique Music (ASCAP).

Looft, W.R. (1971a) Vocational aspirations of second-grade girls, *Psychological Reports*, 28, 241–242.

Looft, W.R. (1971b) Sex differences in the expression of vocational aspirations by elementary school children, *Developmental Psychology*, 5, 366.

Luber, R.L. (1976) Evaluation of poetic mood with the semantic differential, *Psychological Reports*, 39, 499–502.

Luber, R.L. (1978) Assessment of mood change as a function of poetry therapy, *Art Psychotherapy*, 5, 211–215.

Mack, J.E. and Hickler, H.H. (1981) *Vivienne: The Life and Suicide of an Adolescent Girl*, Boston, MA: Little, Brown.

Manilow, B. and Anderson, E. (1974) *Sandra*, Kamikaze Music Corp.

Mann, J. (1981) The core of time-limited psychotherapy: time and the central issue, in Budman, S.H., Ed., *Forms of Brief Therapy*, New York: Guilford, pp. 25–43.

Mann, J. and Goldman, R. (1982) *A Case Book in Time-Limited Psychotherapy*, New York: McGraw-Hill.

Masserman, J.H. (1986) Poetry as music, *The Arts in Psychotherapy*, 13, 61–67.

Mathias, B. (1986) Lifting the shade on family violence, *Family Therapy Networker*, 10, 20–29.

Mattes, G.A., Petak-Davis, S., Waronker, J., Goldstein, M., Mays, D.F., and Fink, M. (1986) Predictors of benefit from art, movement, and poetry therapy: a pilot study, *The Psychiatric Hospital*, 17, 87–90.

Mazza, N. (1979) Poetry: a therapeutic tool in the early stages of alcoholism treatment, *Journal of Studies on Alcohol*, 40(1), 123–128.

Mazza, N. (1981a) The use of poetry in treating the troubled adolescent, *Adolescence*, 16(62), 403–408.

Mazza, N. (1981b) Poetry and Group Counseling: An Exploratory Study, doctoral dissertation, Florida State University, *Dissertation Abstracts International*, 42(6), 2305A.

Mazza, N. (1986) Poetry and popular music in social work education: the liberal arts perspective, *The Arts in Psychotherapy*, 13(4), 293–299.

Mazza, N. (1987a) Poetic approaches in brief psychotherapy, *The American Journal of Social Psychiatry*, 7, 81–83.

Mazza, N. (1987b) Editor's note, *Journal of Poetry Therapy*, 1, 3–4.

Mazza, N. (1988a) Poetry and popular music as adjunctive psychotherapy techniques, in Keller, P.A. and Heyman, S.R., Eds., *Innovation in Clinical Practice: A Source Book*, Vol. 7, Sarasota, FL: Resource Exchange, Inc., pp. 485–494.

Mazza, N. (1988b) The therapeutic use of poetry with the elderly, *Clinical Gerontologist*, 7, 81–85.

Mazza, N. (1989) Poetry and therapy: preventing adolescent suicide, in Deats, S. and Lenker, L., Eds., *Youth Suicide Prevention: Lessons from Literature*, New York: Plenum Press, pp. 49–67.

Mazza, N. (1991a) Adolescence: crisis and loss, in Lerner, A. and Mahlendorf, U., Eds., *Life Guidance through Literature*, Chicago, IL: American Library Association, pp. 110–121.

Mazza, N. (1991b) When victims become survivors: poetry and battered women, in Deats, S.M. and Lenker, L.T., Eds., *The Aching Hearth: Family Violence in Life and Literature*, New York: Plenum Press, pp. 33–50.

Mazza, N. (1993) Poetry therapy: toward a research agenda for the 1990's, *The Arts in Psychotherapy*, 20(1), 51–59.

Mazza, N. (1995a) Sibling ceremony, *Texas Counseling Association Journal*, 23(2), 58.

Mazza, N. (1995b) A certain peace, *Journal of Humanistic Education and Development*, 34, 92.

Mazza, N. (1996) Poetry therapy: a framework and synthesis of techniques for family social work, *Journal of Family Social Work*, 1(3), 3–18.

Mazza, N. (1998a) Hope, *Journal of Humanities Education and Development*, 36, 257.

Mazza, N. (1998b) The place of poetry in gerontological social work education, *Journal of Aging and Identity*, 3, 25–34.

Mazza, N. (1998c) The use of simulations, writing assignments, and assessment measures in family social work education, *Journal of Family Social Work*, 3(1), 71–83.

Mazza, N. (1999) The poetic in family social work, *Journal of Family Social Work*, 4(1), in press.

Mazza, N., Magaz, C., and Scaturro, J. (1987) Poetry therapy with abused children, *The Arts in Psychotherapy*, 14, 85–92.

Mazza, N. and Mazza, J. (1982) Elementary school children and career fantasy: patterns, procedures, and implications, *Viewpoints in Teaching and Learning*, 58, 6–14.

Mazza, N. and Prescott, B.U. (1981) Poetry: an ancillary technique in couples group therapy, *American Journal of Family Therapy*, 9, 53–57.

Mazza, N. and Price, B.D. (1985) When time counts: poetry and music in short-term group treatment, *Social Work with Groups*, 8, 53–66.

McAdams, D. (1993) *The Stories We Live by: Personal Myths and the Making of the Self*, New York: William Morrow.

McKinney, F. (1976) Free writing as therapy, *Psychotherapy: Theory, Research and Practice*, 13, 183–187.

McMahan, M. and Patton, W. (1997) Gender differences in children's and adolescents' perceptions of influences on their career development, *School Counselor*, 44, 368–376.

McNiff, S. (1981) *The Arts and Psychotherapy*, Springfield, IL: Charles C Thomas.

Meeks, E.K. (1959) *The Hill that Grew*, Chicago, IL: Follett.

Mercer, L.E. (1993) Self-healing through poetry writing, *Journal of Poetry Therapy*, 6, 161–168.

Miller, M. (1982) *Suicide Information Center Training Workshop Outline*, San Diego, CA: Suicide Information Center.

Mince, J. (1992) Discovering meaning with families, in Atwood, J.D., Ed., *Family Therapy: A Systemic-Behavioral Approach*, Chicago, IL: Nelson-Hall, pp. 321–343.

Monk, G., Winslade, J., Crocket, K., and Epston, D., Eds. (1997) *Narrative Therapy in Practice: The Archaeology of Hope*, San Francisco, CA: Jossey-Bass.

Montgomery, J.J. and Graham-Pole, J. (1997) A conversation: humanizing the encounter between physician and patient through journalized poetry, *Journal of Poetry Therapy*, 11, 103–111.

Moos, R.H., Insel, D.M., and Humphrey, B. (1974) *Family, Work and Group Environment Scales*, Palo Alto, CA: Consulting Psychologists Press.

Moreno, J. (1946, 1948, 1969) *Psychodrama* (3 vols.), New York: Beacon House.

Morrison, M.R. (1969) Poetry therapy with disturbed adolescents, in Leedy, J.J., Ed., *Poetry Therapy: The Use of Poetry in the Treatment of Emotional Disorders*, Philadelphia, PA: Lippincott, pp. 88–103.

Morrison, M.R., Ed. (1973) A defense of poetry therapy, in Leedy, J.J., Ed., *Poetry the Healer*, Philadelphia, PA: Lippincott, pp. 77–90.

Murray, E.J. and Segal, D.L. (1994) Emotional processing in vocal and written expression of feelings about traumatic experiences, *Journal of Traumatic Stress*, 7, 391–405.

Myers, J.E. (1989) *Adult Children and Aging Parents*, Alexandria, VA: American Counseling Association.

Naitove, C.E. (1982) Art therapy with sexually abused children, in Sgroi, S.M., Ed., *Handbook of Clinical Interventions in Child Sexual Abuse*, Lexington, MA: Lexington Books, pp. 269–308.

National Association of Poetry Therapy (NAPT) (1999) http://www.poetrytherapy.org

National Coalition for Arts Therapies (NACATA) (1999) http://www.membrane.com/ncata

Nemoianu, V.P. (1993) Romanticism, in Preminger, A. and Brogan, T.V.F., Eds., *The New Princeton Encyclopedia of Poetry and Poetics*, Princeton, NJ: Princeton University Press, pp. 1092–1097.

Nichols, M.P. and Zax, M. (1977) *Catharsis in Psychotherapy*, New York: Gardner.

Nunally, E. and Lipchick, E. (1990) Some uses of writing in solution focused brief therapy, *Journal of Independent Social Work*, 4, 5–19.

O'Dell, L. (1984) A bibliotherapist's perspective, in Burnside, I., Ed., *Working with the Elderly: Group Process and Techniques*, 2nd ed., Monterey, CA: Wadsworth, pp. 410–425.

Papp, P. (1984) The creative leap: the links between clinical and artistic creativity, *Family Therapy Networker*, 8, 20–29.

Pardeck, J.T. and Pardeck, J.A. (1987) Using bibliotherapy to help children cope with the changing family, *Social Work in Education*, 9, 107–116.

Parker, R.S. (1969) Poetry as therapeutic art, in Leedy, J.J., Ed., *Poetry Therapy: The Use of Poetry in the Treatment of Emotional Disorders*, Philadelphia, PA: Lippincott, pp. 155–170.

Patterson, J.E. and van Meir, E. (1996) Using patient narratives to teach psychopathology, *Journal of Marital and Family Therapy*, 22, 59–68.

Pattison, E.M. (1973) The psychodynamics of poetry by patients, in Leedy, J.J., Ed., *Poetry the Healer*, Philadelphia, PA: Lippincott, pp. 197–214.

Paul, G. (1967) Outcome research in psychotherapy, *Journal of Consulting Psychology*, 31, 109–118.

Pearce, S.S. (1996) *Flash of Insight: Metaphor and Narrative in Therapy*, Boston, MA: Allyn & Bacon.

Pearson, L., Ed. (1965) *The Use of Written Communications in Psychotherapy*, Springfield, IL: Charles C Thomas.

Peck, C.F. (1989) *From Deep Within: Poetry Workshops in Nursing Homes*, New York: Haworth Press.

Pennebaker, J.W. (1993) Putting stress into words: health, linguistic, and therapeutic implications, *Behavioral Research and Therapy*, 31, 539–548.

Pennebaker, J.W., Mayne, T., and Francis, M. (1997) Linguistic predictors of adaptive bereavement, *Journal of Personality and Social Psychology*, 72, 863–871.

Perls, F.S., Hefferline, R.F., and Goodman, P. (1971) *Gestalt Therapy: Excitement and Growth in the Human Personality*, New York: Julian Press (original work published in 1951).

Pickerill, M. (1993) *Ghostwriter: Family Time*, New York: Children's Television Workshop.

Piercy, M. (1985) Does the light fail us, or do we fail the light?, in *My Mother's Body*, New York: Alfred A. Knopf, pp. 98–104.

Pietropinto, A. (1973) Exploring the unconscious through nonsense poetry, in Leedy, J.J., Ed., *Poetry the Healer*, Philadelphia, PA: Lippincott, pp. 50–76.

Plasse, B.R. (1995) Poetry therapy in a parenting group for recovering addicts, *Journal of Poetry Therapy*, 8, 135–142.

Porter, F.S., Blick, L.C., and Sgroi, S.M. (1982) Treatment of the sexually abused child, in Sgroi, S.M., Ed., *Handbook of Clinical Interventions in Child Sexual Abuse*, Lexington, MA: Lexington Books, pp. 109–145.

Prescott, F.C. (1922) *The Poetic Mind*, New York: Macmillan.

Progoff, I. (1975) *At a Journal Workshop: The Basic Text and Guide for Using the Intensive Journal*, New York: Dialogue House.

Putzel, J. (1975) Toward Alternative Theories of Poetry Therapy, doctoral dissertation, University of Massachussetts, *Dissertation Abstracts International*, 36, 3012B–3013B.

Reich, J. and Neenan, P. (1986) Principles common to different short-term psychotherapies. *American Journal of Psychotherapy*, 40, 62–69.

Reid, W.J. (1978) *The Task-Centered System*, New York: Columbia University Press.

Reiter, S. (1994) Enhancing the quality of life for the frail elderly: Rx, the poetic prescription, *Journal of Long-Term Home Health Care*, 13, 12–19.

Reiter, S. (1997) *Twenty-Two Tried and True All-Time Favorite Poems of Poetry Therapists*, unpublished manuscript.

Rico, G. (1983) *Writing the Natural Way*, Boston: J.P. Tarcher.

Robinson, S.S. and Mowbray, J.K. (1969) Why poetry?, in Leedy, J.J., Ed., *Poetry Therapy: The Use of Poetry in the Treatment of Emotional Disorders*, Philadelphia, PA: Lippincott, pp. 188–199.

Roethke, T. (1953/1990) The waking, in McClatchey, J.D., Ed., *The Vintage Book of Contemporary American Poetry*, New York: Vintage Books, p. 47.

Roethke, T. (1970) My papa's waltz, in Dore, A., Ed., *The Premier Book of Major Poets*, Greenwich, CT: Fawcett, pp. 138–139 (original work published in 1942).

Rolfs, A.M. and Super, S.I. (1988) Guiding the unconscious: the process of poem selection for poetry therapy groups, *The Arts in Psychotherapy*, 15, 119–126.

Roosevelt, G. (1982) An Examination of the Effects of Prepared "Deep Level" Poems Versus "Surface Level" Poems in Poetry Therapy, unpublished doctoral dissertation, International College.

Roscoe, B., Krieg, K., and Schmidt, J. (1985) Written forms of self-expression utilized by adolescents, *Adolescence*, 20, 841–844.

Rose, S.R. (1985) Time-limited groups for children, *Social Work with Groups*, 8, 17–27.

Rosenthal, D.A. and Chapman, D.C. (1980) Sex-role stereotypes: children's perceptions of occupational competence, *Psychological Reports*, 46, 135–139.

Rossiter, C. and Brown, R. (1988) An evaluation of interactive bibliotherapy in a clinical setting, *Journal of Poetry Therapy*, 1, 157–168.

Rossiter, C., Brown, R., and Gladding, S.T. (1990) A new criterion for selecting poems for use in poetry therapy, *Journal of Poetry Therapy*, 4, 5–11.

Rubin, R.J. (1978a) *Using Bibliotherapy: A Guide to Theory and Practice*, Phoenix, AZ: Oryx Press.

Rubin, R.J., Ed. (1978b) *Bibliotherapy Sourcebook*. Phoenix, AZ: Oryx Press.

Rutherford, M. and Robertson, B.A. (1988/1989) *The Living Years*, Hidden Pun Music (BMI).

Satir, V. (1975) I am me, in *Self-Esteem*, Millbrae, CA: Celestial Arts.

Saunders, K. (1983) *Gift of the Strangers (Creativity: A Force for Change)*, Hancock, WI: Pearl-Win.

Schauffler, R.H. (1925) *The Poetry Cure: A Pocket Medicine Chest of Verse*, New York: Dodd, Mead & Co.

Schauffler, R.H. (1931) *The Junior Poetry Cure: A First-Aid Kit of Verse for the Young of All Ages*, New York: Dodd, Mead & Co.

Schloss, G.A. (1976) *Psychopoetry: A New Approach to Self-Awareness Through Poetry Therapy*, New York: Grosset and Dunlap.

Schloss, G.A. and Grundy, D.E. (1978) Action techniques in psychopoetry, in Lerner, A., Ed., *Poetry in the Therapeutic Experience*, New York: Pergamon Press, pp. 81–96.

Schlossberg, N.K. (1990) Training counselors to work with older adults, *Generations*, 14, 7–10.

Schneider, K.J. (1998) Toward a science of the heart: romanticism and the revival of psychology, *American Psychologist*, 53, 277–289.

Sewell, M., Ed. (1991) *Cries of the Spirit: A Celebration of Women's Spirituality*, Boston: Beacon.

Sgroi, S.M.(1982) *Handbook of Clinical Interventions in Child Sexual Abuse*, Lexington, MA: Lexington Books.

Shaffer, J.B.P. and Galinsky, M.D. (1989) *Models of Group Therapy*, Englewood Cliffs, NJ: Prentice-Hall.

Sharlin, S.A. and Shenhar, A. (1986) The fusion of pressing situation and releasing writing: on adolescent suicide poetry, *Suicide and Life-Threatening Behavior*, 16, 343–355.

Shaw, J. (1981) Adolescence, mourning and creativity, *Adolescent Psychiatry*, 9, 60–77.

Shaw, M. (1993) How Metaphoric Interpretations Effect Dynamic Insight: Development of a Model To Represent How Metaphoric Interpretations Effect Dynamic Insight in Psychotherapy Patients, doctoral dissertation, California School of Professional Psychology-Los Angeles, *Dissertation Abstracts International*, 54, 510B.

Shoffstall, V.A. (1971) *After a While*, unpublished poem.

Shrodes, C. (1949) Bibliotherapy: A Theoretical and Clinical Experimental Study, unpublished doctoral dissertation, University of California, Berkeley, 1949.

Silvermarie, S. (1988) Poetry therapy with frail elderly in a nursing home, *Journal of Poetry Therapy*, 2, 72–83.

Silverstein, S. (1974) Treehouse, in *Where the Sidewalk Ends*, New York: Harper & Row, p. 79.

Simon, P. (1964) *The Sounds of Silence*, Charing Cross Music (BMI).

Sloman, L. and Pipitone, J. (1991) Letter writing in family therapy, *American Journal of Family Therapy*, 19, 77–82.

Smyth, J.M. (1998) Written emotional expression: effect sizes, outcome types, and moderating variables, *Journal of Consulting and Clinical Psychology*, 66, 174–184.

Spera, S.P., Buhrfeind, E.D., and Pennebaker, J.W. (1994) Expressive writing and coping with job loss, *Academy of Management Journal*, 37, 722–733.

Stember, C.J. (1977) Printmaking with abused children: a first step in art therapy, *American Journal of Art Therapy*, 16, 104–109.

Stiles, C.G. (1995) How to make a hill: a narrative perspective in special education, *Journal of Poetry Therapy*, 9, 89–91.

Sue, S., Zane, N., and Young, K. (1994) Research on psychotherapy with culturally diverse populations, in Bergin, A.E. and Garfield, S.L., Eds., *Handbook of Psychotherapy and Behavior Change*, 4th ed., New York: John Wiley & Sons, pp. 783–817.

Super, D.E. (1957) *The Psychology of Careers*, New York: Harper & Row.

Swick, K.J. and Carlton, M.E. (1974) An examination of occupational interest of kindergarten children: implications for curriculum development, *Reading Improvement*, 11, 58–61.

Thomas, D. (1952/1970) Do not go gentle into that good night, in Dore, A., Ed., *The Premier Book of Major Poets*, Greenwich, CT: Fawcett, p. 47.

Thompson, C.L. and Rudolph, L.B. (1992) *Counseling Children*, 3rd ed., Pacific Grove, CA: Brooks/Cole.

Torre, E. (1990) Drama as a consciousness-raising strategy for the self-empowerment of working women, *AFFILIA: Journal of Women and Social Work*, 5, 49–65.

Tyson, K.B. (1992) A new approach to relevant scientific research for practitioners: the heuristic paradigm, *Social Work*, 37, 541–556.

Ucko, L.G. (1991) Who's afraid of the big bad wolf? Confronting wife abuse through folk stories, *Social Work*, 36, 414–419.

Vezner, J. and Henry, D. (1989) *Where've You Been?*, Wrensong Pub/Cross Key Don Pub/Tree Group.

Viorst, J. (1971) *The Tenth Good Thing About Barney*, New York: Macmillan.

Vondracek, S.E. and Kirchner, E.P. (1974) Vocational development in early childhood: an examination of young children's expression of vocational aspirations, *Journal of Vocational Behavior*, 5(5), 251–260.

Walker, A. (1968/1991) Medicine, in Sewell, M., Ed., *Cries of the Spirit: A Celebration of Women's Spirituality*, Boston, MA: Beacon, pp. 51–52.

Walker, A. (1979) Good night, Willie Lee, I'll see you in the morning, in *Good Night, Willie Lee, I'll See You in the Morning: Poems by Alice Walker*, San Diego, CA: Harcourt Brace Jovanovich, p. 53.

Walker, A. (1984) How poems are made/a discredited view, in *Horses Make a Landscape Look More Beautiful: Poems*, New York: Harcourt Brace Jovanovich, pp. 17–18..

Walker, L.E. (1979) *The Battered Woman*, New York: Harper & Row.

Walker, L.E. (1984) *The Battered Woman Syndrome*, New York: Springer.

Walker, L.E. (1987) Assessment and intervention with battered women, in Keller, P.A. and Hyman, S.R., Eds., *Innovations in a Clinical Practice: A Source Book*, Vol. 6, Sarasota, FL: Professional Resource Exchange, pp. 131–142.

Watson, J. and Blades, J. (1985) *Goodbye*, Kid Bird Music/Rough Play Music.

Webber, A.L., Eliot, T.S., and Nunn, T. (1982) *Memory*, Koppelman-Bandier Music Corp. (BMI).

Weinger, S. (1998) Children living in poverty: their perceptions of career opportunities, *Families in Society*, 79, 320–330.

Weller, P. and Golden, L.G. (1993) Catharsis, in Preminger, A. and Brogan, T.V.F., Eds., *The New Princeton Encyclopedia of Poetry and Poetics*, Princeton, NJ: Princeton University Press, pp. 175–176.

Wells, R.A. (1994) *Planned Short-Term Treatment*, 2nd ed., New York: Free Press.

Wenz, K. and McWhirter, J.J. (1990) Enhancing the group experience: creative writing exercises, *Journal for Specialists in Group Work*, 15, 37–42.

Whitaker, L.L. (1992) Healing the mother/daughter relationship through the therapeutic use of fairy tales, poetry, and short stories, *Journal of Poetry Therapy*, 6, 35–44.

White, M. and Epston, D. (1990) *Narrative Means to Therapeutic Ends*, New York: Norton.

Whitmont, E.C. and Kaufman, Y. (1973) *Analytical Psychotherapy*, in Corsini, R., Ed., *Current Psychotherapies*, Itasca, IL: F.E. Peacock, pp. 85–117.

Widroe, H. and Davidson, J. (1961) The use of directed writing in psychotherapy, *Bulletin of the Menninger Clinic*, 25, 110–119.

Williams, C.K. (1987/1990) Alzheimer's: the wife, in McClatchey, J.D., Ed., *The Vintage Book of Contemporary American Poetry*, New York: Vintage Books, p. 433.

Williams, M. (1975) *The Velveteen Rabbit*, New York: Avon.

Williams, M.B. (1992) Verbalizing silent screams: the use of poetry to identify the belief systems of adult survivors of childhood sexual abuse, *Journal of Poetry Therapy*, 5, 5–20.

Williams, W.C. (1939/1966) The last words of my English grandmother, in Rose, M.L., Ed., *The William Carlos Williams Reader*, New York: New Directions, p. 60.

Winchester, C.T. (1916) *Some Principles of Literary Criticism*, London: Macmillan.

Winkelman, N.W. and Saul, S.D. (1974) The return of suggestion, *Psychiatric Quarterly*, 48, 230–238.

Witkin, S.L. (1989) Toward a scientific social work, *Journal of Social Service Research*, 12, 83–98.

Witkin, S.L. (1995) Family social work: a critical constructionist perspective, *Journal of Family Social Work*, 1(1), 33–45.

Wohl, A. and Kaufman, B. (1985) *Silent Screams and Hidden Cries: An Interpretation of Artwork by Children from Violent Homes*, New York: Brunner/Mazel.

Wolberg, L. (1965) Methodology in short-term therapy, *American Journal of Psychiatry*, 122, 135–140.

Yalom, I.D. (1995) *The Theory and Practice of Group Psychotherapy*, 4th ed., New York: Basic Books.

Yochim, K. (1994) The collaborative poem and inpatient group therapy: a brief report, *Journal of Poetry Therapy*, 7, 145–149.

Zausner, T. (1997) Division 10: History, scholarship, and activities, *Psychology and the Arts*, Summer, 4.

Zinker, J. (1977) *Creative Process in Gestalt Therapy*, New York: Random House.

Zuniga, M.E. (1992) Using metaphors in therapy: *dichos* and Latino clients, *Social Work*, 37, 55–60.

Appendices

appendix A

Poetry therapy training exercise for practitioners

To use poetry and other forms of literature effectively in therapy, it is imperative for practitioners to first examine their own reactions to the material. The following questions were designed to be used in a self-teaching capacity or in individual and group supervision. Write down responses to the questions for each of the poems provided in Appendix B.

1. What is your personal reaction to this poem?
2. How does this poem relate to what is going on in your life?
3. Is there a theme or message in this poem? If so, please identify it and discuss.
4. Is there a predominant mood in this poem? If so, please identify it and discuss.
5. Is there a particular line or image that has special significance for you?
6. Is there a particular type of client (based on age, gender, or ethnicity) with whom this poem would be helpful?
7. What types of problems could this poem address (e.g., depression, anxiety)?
8. Is there a part of this poem that you would like to change? If so, please do.
9. Does this poem remind you of a song, movie, or other piece of literature? If so, please identify.
10. Draw a picture in response to the poem.
11. Through physical enactment or dance, interpret what this poem means to you.
12. If you could write a letter to the poet, what would you say?
13. Can you identify a psychological theory to match this poem?
14. Can you identify any potential harmful effects in using this poem with a client?
15. Is this poem open ended or prescriptive?
16. Is there "hope" in this poem? Explain.

appendix B

Sample poems for use in poetry therapy

Focus on children

Treehouse
A treehouse, a free house,
A secret you and me house,
A high up in the leafy branches
Cozy as can be house.

A street house, a neat house,
Be sure and wipe your feet house
Is not my kind of house at all...
Let's go live in a tree house.
—Shel Silverstein (from *Where the Sidewalk Ends*, New York Harper Collins, 1974. With permission.)

Climbing
High up in the apple tree climbing I go,
With the sky above me, the earth below.
Each branch is the step of a wonderful stair
Which leads to the town I see shining up there.

Climbing, climbing, higher and higher,
The branches blow and I see a spire,
The gleam of a turret, the glint of a dome,
All sparkling and bright, like white sea foam.

On and on, from bough to bough,
The leaves are thick, but I push my way through;
Before, I have always had to stop,
But today I am sure I shall reach the top.

Today to the end of the marvelous stair,
Where those glittering pinnacles flash in the air!
Climbing, climbing, higher I go,
With the sky close above me, the earth far below.
—Amy Lowell (from *Dome of Many-Coloured Glass*, 1912)

Fringed Gentians
Near where I live there is a lake
As blue as blue can be, winds make
It dance as they go blowing by.
I think it curtseys to the sky.

It's just a lake of lovely flowers
And my Mamma says they are ours;
But they are not like those we grow
To be our very own, you know.

We have a splendid garden, there
Are lots of flowers everywhere;
Roses, and pinks, and four o'clocks
And hollyhocks, and evening stocks.

Mamma lets us pick them, but never
Must we pick any gentians — ever!
For if we carried them away
They'd die of homesickness that day.
—Amy Lowell (from *A Dome of Many-Coloured Glass*, 1912)

Belief/understanding

Who Has Seen the Wind?
Who has seen the wind?
Neither I nor you:
But when the leaves hang trembling,
The wind is passing through.

Who has seen the wind?
Neither you nor I:
But when the trees bow down their heads
The wind is passing by.
—Christina G. Rossetti (1830–1894)

Flower in the Crannied Wall
Flower in the crannied wall,
I pluck you out of the crannies,
I hold you here, root and all, in my hand,
Little flower...but if I could understand
What you are, root and all, and all in all,
I should know what God and man is.
—Alfred, Lord Tennyson (1809–1892)

I Wandered Lonely as a Cloud
I wandered lonely as a cloud
That floats on high o'er vales and hills,
When all at once I saw a crowd,
A host, of golden daffodils;
Beside the lake, beneath the trees,
Fluttering and dancing in the breeze.

Continuous as the stars that shine
And twinkle on the Milky Way,
They stretched in never-ending line
Along the margin of a bay:
Ten thousand saw I at a glance,
Tossing their heads in sprightly dance.

The waves beside them danced; but they
Out-did the sparkling waves in glee:
A poet could not but be gay,
In such a jocund company:
I gazed — and gazed— but little thought
What wealth the show to me had brought:

For oft, when on my couch I lie
In vacant or in pensive mood,
They flash upon that inward eye
Which is the bliss of solitude;
And then my heart with pleasure fills,
And dances with the daffodils.
—William Wordsworth (1770–1850)

Transitions

Petals
Life is a stream
On which we strew
Petal by petal the flower of our heart;
The end lost in dream,
They float past our view,
We only watch their glad, early start.

Freighted with hope,
Crimsoned with joy,
We scatter the leaves of our opening
　　rose;
Their widening scope,
Their distant employ,
We never shall know. And the stream
　　as it flows

Sweeps them away,
Each one is gone
Ever beyond into infinite ways.
We alone stay
While years hurry on,
The flower fared forth, though its fragrance
    still stays.
—Amy Lowell (from *A Dome of Many-Coloured Glass*, 1912)

Winter Has Lasted Too Long
Winter has lasted too long,
    Some dullness refusing to leave.
The nights are too sudden for song,
    The days are too cold to breathe,
Gray branches are staring at me,
    Erasing the memory of Spring,
And we have forgotten the song
    A hummingbird taught us to sing.

Winter has lasted too long,
    The river's too frozen to run.
The sky's a monotonous song
    And daffodils groan for the sun.
We stare at the shivering ground —
    We used to make love in the snow.
Winter has lasted too long!
    I wonder if flowers can grow?

Winter has lasted too long!
    We used to make love in the snow.
Winter has lasted too long!
    I wonder if flowers can grow?
—James Kavanaugh
(from *Winter Has Lasted Too Long*, 1977. Steven J. Nash Publishing Company, P.O. Box 19578, Kalamazoo, MI 49006. With permission.)

Up-Hill
Does the road wind up-hill all the way?
    Yes, to the very end.
Will the day's journey take the whole long day?
    From morn to night, my friend.

But is there for the night a resting-place?
    A roof for when the slow dark hours begin.
May not the darkness hide it from my face?
    You cannot miss that inn.

Shall I meet other wayfarers at night?
  Those who have gone before.
Then must I knock, or call when just in sight?
  They will not keep you standing at the door.

Shall I find comfort, travel-sore and weak?
  Of labour you shall find the sum.
Will there be beds for me and all who seek?
  Yea, beds for all who come.
—Christina Rosetti (1830–1894)

To Everything There Is a Season

To everything there is a season, and a time to every
  purpose under the heaven:
A time to be born, and a time to die; a time to plant,
  and a time to pluck up that which is planted;
A time to kill, and a time to heal; a time to break down,
  and a time to build up;
A time to weep, and a time to laugh; a time to mourn,
  and a time to dance;
A time to cast away stones, and a time to gather stones
  together; a time to embrace, and a time to refrain
  from embracing;
A time to get, and a time to lose; a time to keep, and a
  time to cast away;
A time to rend, and a time to sew; a time to keep
  silence, and a time to speak;
A time to love, and a time to hate; a time of war, and
  a time of peace.
—Ecclesiastes 3:1–8

Friendship/community

I Hear It Was Charged Against Me

I hear it was charged against me that I sought to destroy
  institutions.
But really I am neither for nor against institutions.
(What indeed have I in common with them? or what with
  the destruction of them?)
Only I will establish in the Mannahatta and in every
  city of these States inland and seaboard,
And in the fields and woods, and above every keel little or
  large that dents the water,
Without edifices or rules or trustees or any argument,
The institution of the dear love of comrades.
—Walt Whitman (1819–1892)

To a Friend
I ask but one thing of you, only one,
> *That always you will be my dream of you;*
> *That never shall I wake to find untrue*
All this I have believed and rested on,
Forever vanished, like a vision gone
> *Out into the night. Alas, how few*
> *There are who strike in us a chord we knew*
Existed, but so seldom heard its tone
> *We tremble at the half-forgotten sound.*
The world is full of rude awakenings
> *And heaven-born castles shattered to the ground,*
Yet still our human longing vainly clings
> *To a belief in beauty through all wrongs.*
> *O stay your hand, and leave my heart its songs!*
—Amy Lowell (from *A Dome of Many-Coloured Glass*, 1912)

Grief/loss

From **Macbeth**
Give sorrow words; the grief that does
not speak whispers the oe'r fraught heart
and bids it break.
—William Shakespeare (1564–1616)

From **In Memoriam A.H.H.**
I sometimes hold it half a sin
> *To put in words the grief I feel;*
> *For words, like Nature, half reveal*
And half conceal the Soul within.

But, for the unquiet heart and brain,
> *A use in measured language lies;*
> *The sad mechanic exercise,*
Like dull narcotics, numbing pain.

In words, like weeds, I'll wrap me o'er,
> *Like coarsest clothes against the cold;*
> *But that large grief which these enfold*
Is given in outline and no more.
—Alfred, Lord Tennyson (1809–1892)

Sorrow
Sorrow like a ceaseless rain
> *Beats upon my heart.*
People twist and scream in pain, —
Dawn will find them still again;
This has neither wax nor wane,
> *Neither stop nor start.*

People dress and go to town;
       I sit in my chair.
All my thoughts are slow and brown:
Standing up or sitting down
Little matters, or what gown
       Or what shoes I wear.
—Edna St. Vincent Millay (from *Renascence and Other Poems*, 1917)

Anger

Blight

Hard seeds of hate I planted
       That should by now be grown, —
Rough stalks, and from thick stamens
       A poisonous pollen blown,
And odors rank, unbreathable,
       From dark corollas thrown!

At dawn from my damp garden
       I shook the chilly dew;
The thin boughs locked behind me
       That sprang to let me through;
The blossoms slept, ... I sought a place
       Where nothing lovely grew.

And there, when day was breaking,
       I knelt and looked around:
The light was near, the silence
       Was palpitant with sound;
I drew my hate from out my breast
       And thrust it in the ground.

Oh, ye so fiercely tended,
       Ye little seeds of hate!
I bent above your growing
       Early and noon and late,
Yet are ye drooped and pitiful, —
       I cannot rear ye straight!

The sun seeks out my garden,
       No nook is left in shade,
No mist nor mold nor mildew
       Endures on any blade,
Sweet rain slants under every bough:
       Ye falter, and ye fade.
—Edna St. Vincent Millay (from *Renascence and Other Poems*, 1917)

A Poison Tree
I was angry with my friend:
I told my wrath, my wrath did end.
I was angry with my foe:
I told it not, my wrath did grow.

And I water'd it in fears,
Night & morning with my tears;
And I sunned it with smiles,
And with soft deceitful wiles.

And it grew both day and night,
Till it bore an apple bright;
And my foe beheld it shine,
And he knew that it was mine,

And into my garden stole
When the night had veil'd the pole:
In the morning glad I see
My foe outstretch'd beneath the tree.
—William Blake (1757–1827)

Aging

Terminus
It is time to be old,
To take in sail:
The god of bounds,
Who sets to seas a shore,
Came to me in his fatal rounds,
And said: "No More!"
No farther shoot
Thy broad ambitious branches, and thy root.
Fancy departs: no more invent;
Contract thy firmament
To compass of a tent.
There's not enough for this and that,
Make thy option which of two;
Economize the failing river,
Not the less revere the Giver,
Leave the many and hold the few.
Timely wise accept the terms,
Soften the fall with wary foot;
A little while
Still plan and smile,
And ... fault of novel germs —
Mature the unfallen fruit.

Curse, if though wilt, thy sires,
Bad husbands of their fires,
Who, when they gave thee breath,
Failed to bequeath
The needful sinew stark as once,
The Baresark marrow to thy bones,
But left a legacy of ebbing veins,
Inconstant heat and nerveless reins,
Amid the Muses, left thee deaf and dumb,
Amid the gladiators, halt and numb.

As the bird trims her to the gale,
I trim myself to the storm of time,
I man the rudder, reef the sail,
Obey the voice at eve obeyed at prime:
"Lowly faithful, banish fear,
Right onward drive unharmed;
The port, well worth the cruise, is near,
and every wave is charmed."
—Ralph Waldo Emerson (1803–1882)

Anxiety/decision making

If I Should Cast Off This Tattered Coat
If I should cast off this tattered coat,
And go free into the mighty sky;
If I should find nothing there
But a vast blue,
Echoless, ignorant —
What then?
—Stephen Crane (1871–1900)

When I Have Fears That I May Cease To Be
When I have fears that I may cease to be
Before my pen has glean'd my teeming brain,
Before high-piled books, in charact'ry,
Hold like rich garners the full-ripen'd grain;
When I behold, upon the night's starr'd face,
Huge cloudy symbols of a high romance,
And think that I may never live to trace
Their shadows, with the magic hand of chance;
And when I feel, fair creature of an hour!
That I shall never look upon thee more,
Never have relish in the faery power
Of unreflecting love! — then on the shore
Of the wide world I stand alone, and think
Till love and fame to nothingness do sink.
—John Keats (1795–1821)

Invictus

Out of the night that covers me,
        Black as the Pit from pole to pole,
I thank whatever gods may be
        For my unconquerable soul.
In the fell clutch of circumstance
        I have not winced nor cried aloud.
Under the bludgeonings of change
        My head is bloody, but unbowed.
Beyond this place of wrath and tears
        Looms but the Horror of the shade,
And yet the menace of the years
        Finds, and shall find, me unafraid.
It matters not how strait the gate,
        How charged with punishments the scroll,
I am the master of my fate:
        I am the captain of my soul.
—William Ernest Henley (1849–1903)

Love/relationships

**Though I Speak with the
Tongues of Men and Angels**

Though I speak with the tongues of men and of angels,
        but have not love, I am become as sounding brass,
        or a clanging cymbal.
And though I have the gift of prophecy, and under-
        stand all mysteries, and all knowledge; and though
        I have all faith, so that I could remove mountains,
        but have not love, I am nothing.
And though I bestow all my goods to feed the poor, and
        though I give my body to be burned, and have not
        love, it profiteth me nothing.
Love suffereth long, and is kind; love envieth not; love
        vaunteth not itself, is not puffed up,
Doth not behave itself unseemly, seeketh not her own,
        is not easily provoked, thinketh no evil;
Rejoiceth not in iniquity, but rejoiceth in the truth;
Beareth all things, believeth all things, hopeth all things,
        endureth all things.
Love never faileth: but whether there be prophecies,
        they shall fail; whether there be tongues, they shall
        cease; whether there be knowledge, it shall vanish
        away.

For we know in part, and we prophesy in part.
But when that which is perfect is come, then that
which is in part shall be done away.
When I was a child, I spake as a child, I understood as
a child, I thought as a child: but when I became a
man, I put away childish things.
For now we see through a glass, darkly; but then face
to face: now I know in part; but then shall I know
even as also I am known.
But now abideth faith, hope, love, these three; but the
greatest of these is love.
Corinthians 13:1–13

Crowned
You came to me bearing bright roses,
    Red like the wine of your heart;
You twisted them into a garland
    To set me aside from the mart.
Red roses to crown me your lover,
    And I walked aureoled and apart.

Enslaved and encircled, I bore it,
    Proud token of my gift to you.
The petals waned paler, and shriveled,
    And dropped; and the thorns started through.
Bitter thorns to proclaim me your lover,
    A diadem woven with rue.
—Amy Lowell (from *A Dome of Many-Coloured Glass,* 1912.
Note: This poem is particularly useful in working with sur-
vivors of victimization.)

After a While
After a while you learn the subtle difference
    between holding a hand and chaining a soul
And you learn that love doesn't mean leaning
    and company doesn't always mean security
And you begin to learn that kisses aren't contracts
    and presents aren't promises
And you begin to accept your defeats
    with your head up and your eyes ahead
    with the grace of a woman, not the grief of a child
And you learn to build all your roads on today
    because tomorrow's ground is too uncertain for plans
    and futures have a way of falling down in mid-flight.
After a while you learn that even sunshine burns
    if you get too much.

So you plant your own garden and decorate your own soul
        instead of waiting for someone to bring you flowers.
And you learn that you really can endure
        that you really are strong
        and you really do have worth
And you learn and you learn
        with every goodbye you learn...
—Veronica Shoffstall (©1971 Veronica Shoffstall. Reprinted with permission. *Note:* This poem is particularly useful in working with survivors of victimization.)

Wild Nights...Wild Nights!
Were I with thee
Wild Nights should be
Our luxury!

Futile — the Winds —
To a Heart in port —
Done with the Compass —
Done with the Chart!

Rowing in Eden —
Ah, the Sea!
Might I but moor — Tonight —
In Thee!
—Emily Dickinson (1830–1886)

Identity

We Wear the Mask
We wear the mask that grins and lies
It hides our cheeks and shades our eyes, —
This debt we pay to human guile;
With torn and bleeding hearts we smile,
And mouth with myriad subtleties.

Why should the world be overwise,
In counting all our tears and sighs?
Nay, let them only see us, while
        We wear the mask.

We smile, but, oh great Christ, our cries
To thee from tortured souls arise.
We sing, but oh the clay is vile
Beneath our feet, and long the mile;
But let the world dream otherwise,
        We wear the mask!
—Paul Laurence Dunbar (1872–1906)

Hope

Hope is the thing with feathers
That perches in the soul,
And sings the tune without the words
And never stops at all,

And sweetest in the gale is heard;
And sore must be the storm
That could abash the little bird
That kept so many warm.

I've heard it in the chillest land,
And on the strangest sea;
Yet, never, in extremity,
It asked a crumb of me.
—Emily Dickinson (1830–1886)

From **Ulysses**

The lights begin to twinkle from the rocks:
The long day wanes: the slow moon climbs: the deep
Moans round with many voices. Come, my friends,
'Tis not too late to seek a newer world.

Push off, and sitting well in order smite
The sounding furrows; for my purpose holds
To sail beyond the sunset, and the baths
Of all the western stars, until I die.
—Alfred, Lord Tennyson (1809–1892)
(In memory of Robert F. Kennedy and Harry Chapin. —NM)

appendix C

Poetic stems

The following generic sentence stems can be used to promote client verbalization, writing, and/or nonverbal expression. Please note that a number of these stems have been modified and used in unique sequences for particular educational and/or clinical purposes by various authors/practitioners.

If you knew me...

I am most happy when...

I am most sad when...

I believe...

I feel loved when...

I am afraid of...

I am angry about...

I am doubtful about...

I am hurt when...

I am...

If you said no...

If you said yes...

If you ignored me...

When I am alone...

When I am in a crowd...

If my hands could speak...

I care about...

Yesterday, I was...

Today, I am...

Tomorrow, I...

Hope is...

Fear is...

Anger is...

Happiness is...

Despair is...

Intimacy is...

Love is...

Home is...

In a forest, I am...

In a shopping mall, I am...

I keep on because...

What matters most is...

I feel closest to...

I stand for...

My greatest strength is...

appendix D

Poetry therapy narrative report for group work: guidelines

The purpose of the narrative report is to provide descriptive information about the use of poetry in group counseling. Your impressions and clinical observations are of primary importance. Some of the specific areas to consider include:

1. How did the group leader introduce the poem? That is, did he or she connect the poem to something a member mentioned, relate it to a mood or feeling in the group, simply express it as a wish to share the poem, etc.?
2. How did the group respond to the poem? Was there initial silence, intellectualization, confusion, insight, affect? Remember to consider both verbal and nonverbal responses.
3. Were there any lines in the poem that had a special effect?
4. How did the group leader initiate the collaborative poem?
5. Describe the collaborative poem (e.g., how indicative of group mood it was, members' attitude in constructing it, what it accomplished, etc.).
6. How much time (approximate minutes) was spent on poetry exclusively?
7. What are the principal advantages of using this technique?
8. What are the principal disadvantages of using this technique?
9. Can you think of any poems (or song lyrics) that you would have used in this session?
10. What questions do you have about what you observed?
11. What do you think the use of a preexisting poem accomplished?
12. What do you think the use of the collaborative poem accomplished?

appendix E

Poetry therapy narrative report for group work: observer form

Observer _____ Date _____ Group _____

Poetry Therapy Narrative Report — Observer Form

Collaborative poem from previous week

Introduced _____ minutes into session.

Discussed poem directly for _____ minutes.

Comments:

_____

_____

_____

Preexisting poem utilized (title: _____)

Introduced _____ minutes into session.

Discussed poem directly for _____ minutes.

Comments:

_____

_____

_____

Collaborative poem

Introduced _____ minutes into session.

Constructed and discussed poem for _____ minutes.

Poem (verbatim; circle the words which the leader contributed):

_____

_____

_____

_____

_____

_____

_____

_____

Comments:

_____

_____

_____

General impressions (use separate sheet if necessary):

_____

_____

_____

Poetry therapy narrative report for group work: leader form

Leader _____ Date _____ Group _____

Poetry Therapy Narrative Report — Leader Form

Collaborative poem from previous week

_____

Comments:

_____

_____

_____

Preexisting poem utilized (title: _____)

Why?

_____

_____

Comments:

_____

_____

_____

Collaborative poem

Poem (verbatim; circle the words which you contributed):

_____

_____

_____

_____

_____

_____

_____

_____

Comments:

_____

_____

_____

General impressions (include any questions you may have):

_____

_____

_____

Plan:

_____

_____

_____

Writing exercise

The following creative writing exercise is from Goldberg (1986):

Creating action in a sentence: Take a sheet of paper and fold it vertically. On the left side of the sheet, list any ten nouns. For example:

Horse	Rose
Car	Chair
Door	Shirt
Candle	Book
Flashlight	Dog

On the right side of the sheet, think of an occupation or career and list 15 verbs to fit the position. For example, a carpenter:

Cut	Screw	Chip
Hammer	Glue	Join
Measure	Climb	Assemble
Sand	Lift	Fit
Stack	Plan	Drill

Open the sheet and try to link the nouns and verbs (any tense permitted) to form a sentence. For example:

> The dog assembled my chair.
>
> I lifted a candle.

Note that this exercise has the potential to generate sentences reflecting a wide range of emotions.

appendix H

The AIDS poetry
project workbook*

The AIDS Poetry Project is a not-for-profit project founded by HIV-positive poet, mother, and activist Sandra Vreeland (1958–1996), winner of the Mother's Voices' 1995 Extraordinary Voices award and author of *The Sky Lotto* (Cannio's Editions, 1995). The goal of the project is to encourage young people to express their thoughts and feelings about AIDS in poetry and, through these poems, to share their wisdom with the world. Through a volunteer network of teachers, writers, counselors, and others, the AIDS Poetry Project has collected poetry from young people ages 6 to 18 from across the nation.

Understanding

Virus
It's there when you are,
you can't see it,
but it can see you,
you can't touch it
but it can touch you,
you can't stop it,
but it can stop you,
you can't hear it,
but it can hear you,
you can't smell it,
but it can smell you,
you can't kill it,
but it can kill you.
AIDS.
Dedicated to those who have died and those who will.
by Alex Michaels, age 13

---

* Reprinted with permission from Susan Sully, The AIDS Poetry Project; http://www.thebody.com/poetryproj/workbook2.html.)

175

AIDS
Acquired Immune Deficiency Syndrome
To some, AIDS means —
There is no hope for me.
It's time to write my will.
It's time to say goodbye.
It's time to die.
They feel angry.
They feel scared.
Even sorry for themselves.
And to some, AIDS means —
It's time to enjoy life the best way I can.
It's time to tell my friends and family how much I love
*   them and how I really feel.*
Some feel happy with the life they have lived so far.
Happy to have their loved ones by their side.
Happy to have loved.
To know and love someone with AIDS.
To go through it all
Is almost the same as having AIDS —
Not physically, but mentally.
AIDS isn't a punishment, but
A lesson that the whole world is
Learning at the same time.
by Sally Montas, age 17

Writing exercises for understanding

1. Write a poem answering the question, "What is AIDS/HIV?" Don't just define the disease. What is it like? What does it taste like? Look like? Smell like? Where did it come from? What lessons is AIDS teaching the world — such as learning to help each other or learning how to live with the knowledge that you may die soon?

2. Imagine that you are the AIDS/HIV virus: Who are you? What do you look like? What do you sound like? Why did you come here? What do you want?

3. Write a poem that creates a simile for AIDS. A simile is a figure of speech that compares something to other things (using "like" or "as") in order to provide new insights into the nature of that thing. A good example is the following line from a poem: "My love is like a red, red rose." This statement tells us that love is beautiful, bright, and perhaps fleeting, because a rose does not bloom forever. What is AIDS like?

Communication

I Love You
AIDS — to possess it — I don't know
To be scared of dying, I do.
Knowing tomorrow could be the end
And I might have to say goodbye
Before you say good night
You say Mommy, Daddy, brother, sister, friend,
I love you.
You don't know if they will be the
last words that could come out of your mouth
or the last chance to tell them
you love them.
Tears running down.
Put your hands together and pray.
I don't have AIDS or any disease.
But I'm scared of dying and scared of losing.
I want to keep telling them I love them.
by Nina Gribetz, age 12

Fading Light
My heart is hopeful
my hands are full of dreams
the thought of leaving is
harder than
it seems
Robin —
You are my life and without you
I would not mind
dying.
The last touch of your face
flashes through
my ephemeral life
The moonlight is
fading,
And the flowers are
wilting.
My body grows
weaker under
the sheet.
The burning
light is
still in your
heart

as my light
grows
dim.
This deadly gift
is all that is
left of
me.
And then wherever it is
I will see
you again.
— Chris
by Allysan Gerstein, age 16

Writing exercises for communication

1. Imagine that you have AIDS/HIV, but you have kept it a secret. Write a poem explaining why you have kept this secret. What are you afraid will happen if you tell people that you have AIDS? What are the consequences of this decision? Are you putting others at risk? Are you cutting yourself off from the love and understanding of others? Imagine that you told your secret. What unexpected things might happen? What good would come of telling your secret?

2. Think of someone you love. What would you want to tell this person if he or she just told you that he or she had just been diagnosed with AIDS/HIV? Would you comfort the person? Would you offer words of hope? What advice would you give? Now, write a poem in the form of a letter or a conversation. Or just describe this interchange between you and someone you love.

3. Imagine that you have learned that you are dying. What would you want to say to the people you love most in the world? How would you comfort them? How would you like to be remembered — every time they heard a certain song or ate your favorite food or smelled a special scent? What will you miss most about them or the world? How can they comfort you as you prepare to leave life as you know it and enter into the unknown world of dying?

Compassion

AIDS
AIDS is a sickness.
I feel that people who have AIDS
Are no different than us.
Please take my hand and I will be your friend.

I will find help for you.
I will help you see the light of day, every day.
by Christine Genco, age 12

World of Red
As the red ribbons have become a part of our lives,
    we look, and wonder, and notice, we're concerned.
Walking down the streets as the heads all turn,
    with a sign of affection in one's eyes.
And everyone says that AIDS is not real.
    and AIDS does not discriminate.
Yet we are aware that it is not true,
    for the world is full of prejudice.
But then she's there, you can spot her fast,
    like a star that doesn't shine.
For her body has become a tree in the winter,
    as she begins to diminish as seasons change.
Though she is one that will not reappear,
    but will fade as the years pass on.
It is hard for her in the outside world
    to watch human nature flourish,
    while she is cold and all alone,
    standing outside the window.
There are many thoughts to cross her mind,
    so many goals to conquer,
    for she knows soon it will be too late,
    and death will be commencing.
But once in a while you'll see her there,
    at her favorite bench in the park,
    closing her eyes and trying to dream
    of the life she couldn't possess.
Reality begins at the end of her life,
    when there are no more corners to turn.
Realizing now, and seeing the facts,
    that AIDS is more than real.
by Stacey Druver, age 15

Writing exercises for compassion

1. Imagine that you are living with AIDS/HIV. What is it like to have AIDS? How do you feel physically? Emotionally? Spiritually? Write a poem about this.
2. Why are people not always compassionate to people with AIDS/HIV? Is it because they are afraid of people with AIDS/HIV because they remind them that they, too, may someday get sick

or die? How can people stop being afraid and start becoming more caring? If everyone cared more and was less afraid, would it be a better world? Write a poem about this.

3. Pretend you are a doctor or a nurse who cares for AIDS patients. Describe what it is like caring for someone with AIDS. Is it sad sometimes? Do you ever laugh with your patients about something? Do you cry? What is it like when you go home at the end of the day? What do you learn from your patients? Do you learn things that make life more precious? Describe all of this in a poem.

Grieving

To My Mom in Heaven
If you were a star
I would be the moon
> *so you could see me every night.*
If you were a rainbow
> *after the rain*
I could be the sun
> *so I could talk to you.*
If you were a dandelion
> *growing in the grass*
I would pick you up
> *and make a wish.*
by Jovany, age 13

Stardust
Stardust
an invisible thought
a white light fills
the blackness stood upon
showered by hope
love an apparent ray
when I face you
in your stardust
the man
once known
is now
just stardust
glowing amber mixed
with the twilight
of a blinding
path
clear
skies black

as ebony
spotted with your
stardust
before me
a notion
for your
stardust falls
landing
in my hand
while I
stare
and dream
of your stardust fading into day.
by Jennifer Sandella

Writing exercises for grieving

1. Imagine that you are a child whose mother or father has died from the AIDS virus. Pretend that you are in your bed, thinking of your mother or father and suddenly you feel his or her comforting presence in the room. What is this like? How do you recognize that it is your mother's or father's presence? How do you feel? What do you learn from the experience?

2. Pretend that a good friend of yours has just lost someone to AIDS. What would you say to comfort this person? Write a poem, maybe in the form of a letter, about this.

3. Imagine the feelings of loss or loneliness that come when someone you love dies. What do you miss most about that person? How is the world different now that he or she is no longer alive? How is each day or each night different? What can you do or think to help ease this pain? Describe this in a poem.

4. What would you do if someone you loved dies before you had time to tell him or her something important? Maybe you had an old argument that had never been resolved. Perhaps you didn't have a chance to say "I love you." Maybe you want to tell that person how he or she will have a lasting effect on your life. Write a poem telling this person what you want to say.

Anger

Letting HIV/AIDS Know Something
HIV, you are hurting friends and family.
AIDS, you are killing them.
If only one day we should find
A way to destroy you we would.
by Christian Reyes, Age 17

If I Could

If only you knew how
*   you made me feel inside*
*   the hurt, the anger*
*   but most of all the pain.*
You go around destroying
*   lives taking out all of*
*   my people like a big genocide.*
There are not words
*   that would describe*
*   my pain exactly but*
*   one word I feel towards*
*   you is hate.*
You came into our lives
*   day by day as if what*
*   you do is nothing.*
You're wrong! Dead wrong!
You affect our way of
*   living, you stop us from*
*   achieving our goals.*
You're a killer, a murderer
*   you creep into our system*
*   and use our own bodies*
*   to kill us off.*
Slow and painful that's
*   the way you kill us all.*
My heart can no longer
*   save me. Instead it pumps*
*   blood that helps to kill me.*
You steal our dreams
*   you take our hopes and crush them.*
The anger I had inside
*   for you is not enough.*
So small yet so
*   much damage can you cause*
*   so unnoticeable yet inside*
*   you're raging.*
by Michelle Ortiz, age 17

Writing exercises for anger

1. If you had the AIDS/HIV virus, there would probably be times
   when you felt very angry about being sick. Write a poem about
   this. What can't you do that you used to be able to do? What
   makes you feel different from other people? How do you feel

differently about your future now than you did before your diagnosis? Is there something you can say to make yourself feel less angry? Write a poem about this.

2. Are you angry that someone you know has AIDS/HIV or that AIDS/HIV exists at all? What makes you angry about it? Is it because people you love have gotten sick or died? Is it because you may have to be more careful in order to avoid getting AIDS? Is it because it seems unfair that so many people have had to die young because of this disease? Why are you angry about AIDS? Make a list of these things, then make it into a poem.

3. Imagine that someone you know who has AIDS is feeling very angry. What could you say to him or her? Is it okay to feel angry? Maybe you could help this person express his or her anger creatively — could you yell together? Throw food around the room? Play loud music? Break something? Would there be any-thing funny about this? Would you both end up laughing? Or maybe one of you would begin to cry, and the other might offer sympathy. Write a poem about a situation like this.

Acceptance

Life and AIDS

Life is a beautiful thing,
    sometimes filled with joy and happiness,
    and sometimes, we have pain and sadness.
As we grow, we learn to appreciate the things that are given to us,
    and the things we try hard to achieve.
So too for a baby born with AIDS:
    what is given to them, young and so innocent, is life.
AIDS is not a sin, nor a crime,
    more like a drawback in life.
Try not to look on the dark side of things,
    but on the brighter side.
Don't let it get you down.
Rise up and strive to the best of your abilities.
Enjoy every minute of life, achieve all you can.
by Nadia Morgan, age 16

Writing exercises for acceptance

1. Imagine that you have just been diagnosed with the AIDS virus. How would you deal with this? Would you be angry at first? Or maybe not believe it, or pretend that it was a bad dream? After a while, you would have to come to terms with your disease and find a new way to live with the fact that you have an illness and

might die from it. How would you live your life differently? Would you treat people differently? Would you try to spend your time in different ways? Describe this in a poem.

2. How would you feel if you learned that someone you love has AIDS/HIV? How would you come to terms with the fact that this person might sometimes feel very sick and might even die sooner that you expected? Would you fight this knowledge, pretending that everything was "normal"? After a while, would you accept this knowledge and find a new way to live with it? How would it change the way that you treat this person? Pretend that you are explaining to this person why you have been acting strangely since you found out about his or her diagnosis. Or imagine that you are writing in your journal about his or her experience.

3. Does the world, as a whole, have to accept AIDS as a reality in order to learn how to live with AIDS as a part of life? What does this mean? If we "accept" AIDS, does that mean that we will protect ourselves better so that fewer people will contract the virus? Will "accepting" AIDS mean that more people will work together to find a cure for the disease? Will "accepting" AIDS mean that society will take better care of people who already have the disease? Write a letter to the world explaining why it is better to accept AIDS than to pretend that it doesn't exist.

4. Can you think of at least one good thing about AIDS/HIV? Has it taught us that life is precious? Is it helping to bring people together? Will we live life more fully when we remember that we may die sooner rather than later? Write a poem about this.

Hope

You Can't Stop Me...
I'm just a person, plain to the eye,
Look inside my soul, there's a lot you might find.
Don't be afraid, I won't hurt you, you see,
There's not many differences, between you and me.
I may be sick more often, and won't hesitate to cry,
Sometimes I wake up in the morning, and ask myself why???
Why am I hurting, why must this be?
But for all the obstacles in my way...
YOU CAN'T STOP ME!!!
At night I wake up in a sweat,
Will I live to another day?
I run to the window, look up at the sky, and silently began to pray.
"Dear GOD and all the heavens above, please guard me with your
     light,

And make my body tough and strong, and prepare it for the fight.
See I've just discovered for the past few months, I've been living
   with HIV.
So I'm asking you to heed my words, and put a blessing on my
   heart,
So that I may live a little longer and prevent this from the start.
That's the end of my prayer, and LORD it's not just for me,
But it's for all the people in the world, whose eyes have not yet
   seen."
Sometimes I just stare out the window, and think of how things
   would be,
But for all those thoughts that get me down...
YOU CAN'T STOP ME!!!
by Takesha La'Shawn Rogers, age 17

How I See You
I see you as a touch of light.
Black or white I still see you as a touch of light.
The sign of peace is in your heart.
Eyes of all different colors.
Sun or rain I can see you in the earth.
Because it is in me.
Shiny or dark you are still a touch of light.
Because it is in us.
by Marley Stone, age 8

Writing exercises for hope

1. Create a metaphor for hope. An example of a metaphor is "Life is a joke." Life isn't really a joke, but by saying that it is a joke, we are saying that life is funny or unpredictable, like a joke. What is hope? A flower? A cloud? A sunset? A piece of driftwood? Think of something that makes you think of hope and write a poem that explores this metaphor.
2. Why is hope important? Does hope keep doctors working for a cure? Does hope keep someone who has learned that he or she has AIDS from giving up? Does hope help us cope with the knowledge that someone we love may suffer or die? What would happen if we gave up hope? Think of one way that hope is important, and in a poem explain why it is crucial not to give up hope.
3. When you think about AIDS/HIV, what do you hope for? Is there a person who has AIDS that you hope will live a healthy, happy life? Do you hope for a cure? Do you hope that you won't ever contract AIDS? Do you hope that people who are unhappy

because of AIDS will find comfort and wisdom? What do you hope for? Write a poem about it.

4. Write a four-line poem with each line beginning with the letters H, O, P, E. Have the poem say something about hope, but do not use the word hope in the poem.

appendix I

Resources

Organizations

National Association for Poetry Therapy; 12950 N.W. 5th St., Pembroke
Pines, FL 33028; telephone (toll free): (866) 844-NAPT; e-mail: info@poet-
rytherapy.org; http://www.poetrytherapy.org/

National Coalition of Arts Therapies Associations; 2117L Street, N.W. #274;
Washington, DC 20037; telephone: (202) 678-6787; http://www.ncata.com/

The Center of Journal Therapy; 12477 W. Cedar Dr., #102; Lakewood, CO 80228;
telephone: (888) 421-2298; http://www.journaltherapy.com/

Journals

Journal of Poetry Therapy (quarterly, articles abstracted by ERIC, Current Index to
Journals in Education), MLA, Article First; Previously published by
Kluwer/Human Sciences Press (Vol. 1–Vol. 15). Currently published by the
National Association for Poetry Therapy. Editor: Nicholas Mazza, Ph.D.;
Florida State University School of Social Work; Tallahassee, FL 32306-2570.

The Arts in Psychotherapy (five issues per year, articles abstracted by PsycINFO);
Elsevier Science, Inc.; 655 Avenue of the Americas; New York, NY 10010; telephone 1-888-437-4635. Editor: Irma Dosamantes-Beaudry, Ph.D.; World Arts
and Cultures Dept.; Box 951608; Los Angeles, CA 90095-1608.

Internet

Literature, Arts, and Medicine Database, an annotated bibliography of prose,
poetry, film, video, and art related to medical humanities: http://endeav-
or.med.nyu.edu/lit-med/lit-med-db/

The Poetry Archives, archives of classical poetry: http://www.emule.com/
poetry/

Poetry Society of America: http://www.poetrysociety.org/

Children's Literature and Language Arts Resources: http://falcon.jmu.edu/
~ramsayil/childlit.htm

Project Bartleby, literature in the public domain: http://www.columbia.edu/
acis/bartleby/bartcriteria.html

Project Gutenberg, literature in the public domain: http://www.gutenberg.net/

Poems from the Planet Earth: http://redfrog.norconnect.no/~poems/poems/

National Association for Poetry Therapy Code of Ethics

Preamble

This code is intended to serve as a guide to the everyday conduct of members of the biblio/poetry therapy profession and as a basis for the adjudication of issues in ethics when the conduct of biblio/poetry therapists is alleged to deviate from the standards expressed or implied in this code. It represents standards of ethical behavior in professional relationships with those served, with colleagues, with employers, with other professionals, and with the community.

Principle 1 — responsibility

In providing services, biblio/poetry therapists maintain the highest standards of their profession. They accept responsibility for the consequences of their acts and make every effort to ensure that their services are used appropriately. As practitioners, biblio/poetry therapists know that they bear a heavy social responsibility because their recommendations and professional actions may alter the lives of others.

As educators, biblio/poetry therapists recognize their obligation to help others acquire knowledge and skill.

As researchers, biblio/poetry therapists plan their research in ways to minimize the possibility that their findings will be misleading. In publishing reports of their work, they never suppress disconfirming data, and they acknowledge the existence of alternative hypotheses and explanations of their findings. They take credit only for work they have actually done. Biblio/poetry therapists clarify in advance with all appropriate persons and agencies the expectations for sharing and utilizing research data.

Principle 2 — *competence*

The maintenance of high standards of competence is a responsibility shared by all biblio/poetry therapists in the interest of the public and the profession as a whole. Biblio/poetry therapists recognize the boundaries of their competence and the limitations of their techniques. They only provide services and only use techniques for which they are qualified by training and experience. In those areas in which recognized standards do not yet exist, biblio/poetry therapists take whatever precautions are necessary to protect the welfare of their clients.

Biblio/poetry therapists accurately represent their competence, education, training, and experience. They recognize the need for continuing education and are open to new techniques and materials. They recognize differences among people, such as those associated with age, sex, or socioeconomic and ethnic backgrounds, and when necessary, they obtain training, experience, or counseling to assure competent service or research relating to such persons.

Biblio/poetry therapists recognize that personal problems and conflicts may interfere with professional effectiveness. Accordingly, they refrain from undertaking any activity in which their personal problems are likely to lead to inadequate performance or harm to a client, colleague, student, or research participant.

Principle 3 — *public statements*

In their public statements, announcements of services, advertising, and promotional activities, biblio/poetry therapists represent accurately and objectively their professional qualifications, affiliations, and functions, as well as those of the institutions or organizations with which they may be associated. Announcements or advertisements of personal growth groups, workshops, and other professional activities should give a clear statement of purpose and a clear description of the experiences to be provided.

Principle 4 — *confidentiality*

Biblio/poetry therapists have a primary obligation to respect the confidentiality of information obtained from the persons in the course of their work as therapists. They reveal such information to others only with the consent of the person or the person's legal representative, except in those unusual circumstances in which not doing so would result in clear danger to the person or to others. Where appropriate, biblio/poetry therapists inform their clients of the legal limits of confidentiality.

Information obtained in clinical or consulting relationships can be discussed for professional work in writings, lectures, or other public forums only if adequate prior consent is obtained or if there is adequate disguising of all identifying information.

Principle 5 — *welfare of the client*

Biblio/poetry therapists respect the integrity and protect the welfare of the people and groups with whom they work, and they freely acknowledge that clients, students or participants in research have freedom of choice with regard to participation.

Biblio/poetry therapists are continually cognizant of their own needs and of their potentially influential position *vis-a-vis* persons such as clients, students, and subordinates. They avoid exploiting the trust and dependency of such persons. Biblio/poetry therapists make every effort to avoid dual relationships that could impair their professional judgment or increase the risk of exploitation. Examples of such dual relationships include, but are not limited to, research with or treatment of employees, students, supervisees, close friends, or relatives. Sexual intimacies with clients are unethical.

Biblio/poetry therapists make advance financial arrangements that safeguard the best interests of and are clearly understood by their clients.

Biblio/poetry therapists terminate a clinical or consulting relationship when it is reasonably clear that the consumer is not benefitting from it. They offer to help the consumer locate alternative sources of assistance.

Principle 6 — *professional relationships*

Biblio/poetry therapists act with due regard for the needs, special competencies, and obligations of their colleagues in their own and other professions. They respect the prerogatives and obligations of the institutions or organizations with which these other colleagues are associated.

In conducting research in institutions or organizations, biblio/poetry therapists secure appropriate authorization to conduct such research. They are aware of their obligations to future researchers and ensure that host institutions receive adequate information about the research and proper acknowledgment of their contributions.

Publication credit is assigned to those who have contributed to a publication in proportion to their professional contributions.

When biblio/poetry therapists know of an ethical violation by another biblio/poetry therapist, and it seems appropriate, they informally attempt to resolve the issue by bringing the behavior to the attention of this colleague. If the misconduct is of a minor nature and/or appears to be due to lack of sensitivity, knowledge, or experience, such an informal solution is usually appropriate. Such informal corrective efforts are made with sensitivity to any rights to confidentiality involved. If the violation does not seem amenable to informal solution, or is of a more serious nature, biblio/poetry therapists bring it to the attention of the appropriate committee on professional ethics and conduct.

Index

Index

reason, 4
receptive mode, 24, 68
receptive/prescriptive mode of
    poetry therapy, 17, 33, 34,
    47, 48, 76, 98, 105, 108–111,
    122
  bibliotherapy, traditional, 34
  preexisting poems, use of,
    18–19
redundancy letters, 39
reframing, 33
registered poetry therapist (RPT),
    121
relational psychology, 4
replication of research, 107
research, 105–117
  agenda for poetry therapy,
    115–117
resistance, 25, 34, 72, 98
resource development, 125
resources for poetry therapy, 187
rituals, 17, 22, 40, 100, 106, 122
"Road Not Taken, The", 18, 23,
    25–26, 81, 87, 107, 111
role-playing, 11
romantic poets, 4
RPT. *See* registered poetry
    therapist
Rubin, Rhea J., 8

S

"Sandra", 41
Schauffler, Robert H., 6, 61
schizophrenia, 12
Schloss, Gilbert, 6, 7, 25, 109
scrapbooks, 20
self-confidence, 26
self-exploration, 19
sentence stems, 20, 26, 37–38, 62,
    78, 88, 112, 165
  examples of, 38
separation, in therapy, 30
sessions, pace of, 55
sex therapy, 38

sex-role stereotyping, 64
sexual abuse, 111–112. *See also*
    child abuse, treatment of
Shrodes, Carolyn, 8
sign, definition of, 9
"So You Couldn't Get to Me", 50,
    55, 91
social cognitive theory, 106
social learning theory, 106
"Sometimes When We Touch", 52
songs, 26, 28, 33, 48, 108
  lyrics of, 19, 34–36
  selection of, 19
  table of, 35
  use with adolescents, 76
"Sounds of Silence, The", 44
specificity of research, 107
spouse abuse. *See* women,
    battered
"Stopping by the Woods on a
    Snowy Evening", 110
stories, 12, 13, 20, 40, 98, 100, 108,
    112
storytelling, 17, 22, 33, 40, 47, 100
  by children, 62
strategic family therapy, 33
structural family therapy, 33
subjectivity, 4
suggestion, use of, 24
suicide, adolescent, 75–83
supportive phase, 28
symbol, 12, 21
  definition of, 9
symbolic-experiential family
    therapy, 33
symbolic/ceremonial mode of
    psychotherapy, 17, 21–22,
    33, 40–41, 47, 98, 100, 105,
    113, 122
  metaphors, 40–41
  rituals, 40
  storytelling, 40
symbolization, 9
symbols, 89
systemic family therapy, 33

Made in the USA
San Bernardino, CA
24 February 2018